About the Author

Tony Marshall is a full blooded Romany gypsy, whose ancestry dates back hundreds of years in the UK and the USA. He lives in Essex but at present resides in the UAE. His upbringing is that of the traditional Romany Gypsy life, which he has dragged into the modern world kicking and screaming.

To my wonderful wife Lila, they say behind every great man there is a great woman, I don't consider myself to be great, but I know she is, and my wonderful children and grandchildren who I love with all my heart.

Tony Marshall

THE PRINCE OF GYPSIES

A CIP catalogue record for this title is available from the British Library.

Some of this book is fact, some is fiction: I will leave it to you to decide which is which.

ISBN 978 1 78455 221 3

www.austinmacauley.com

First Published (2014)
Austin Macauley Publishers Ltd.
25 Canada Square
Canary Wharf
London
E14 5LB

Printed and bound in Great Britain

PRELUDE

There have been many accounts documented as to the origins of the Gypsy race, mostly old wives' tales that if believed would have us originating from every corner of the globe, but the true history of our race lies in the name *Gypsy*, a shortened down version of the word 'Egyptians': tales told around camp fires going back centuries are that we came from the lost tribe of Egypt that Moses led across the Red Sea to freedom. This tribe of nomads wandered without settling, thus starting the nomadic culture still beating within every true Romany Gypsy's heart to this day. Gypsies have long been among the most mysterious, exotic peoples on earth, they have been described as a race of nomads, who have no real home; Gypsies do have their own language, Romanice, and they identify themselves as Romany people.

Symon Simeonis describes Gypsies in Crete (1323) as rarely or never stopping in one place beyond 30 days, but always wandering and fugitive, from field to field with their oblong tents, back and low, as if accursed by God.

CHAPTER ONE

EUROPEAN GYPSIES

The first record of Gypsies in Scotland is 1505 as "Tinkers, Peddlers, Dancers and Raconteurs". In 1609, the Vagabonds Act was aimed at Gypsies, and four male members of the Faa family were hung in 1611 for not maintaining a permanent address; eight more men, six of them with the last name Faa, were hanged in 1624 for being "EGYPTIANS". The Faa, Bailey and Marshall names go back centuries in the UK. A new decree was issued in 1624 that traveling Gypsy men be arrested and hanged, Gypsy women without children be drowned, and Gypsy women with children be whipped and branded on the cheek.

In England the Egyptian Act was passed to expel Gypsies from the realm, for being lewd vagabonds. In 1562 Queen Elizabeth signed an order designed to force Gypsies to settle into permanent dwellings, or face death. Several were hanged in 1577 and nine more in 1596, and thirteen in the 1650's. Under King James I, England began to deport Gypsy people to the American colonies, as well as Jamaica and Barbados. Dumping the so-called undesirables into the colonies became widespread practice.

In Spain it seems the Gypsies were welcomed; it is there they first began to be called Bohemians. People flocked to them to have their fortunes told. The Gypsies claimed to have dukes and counts among them, and captains and kings. The Spanish nobility protected them at first: Gypsy women were adored for their beauty and seductive charms, Gypsy men were admired as excellent judges of the quality of horses, and hired by nobles to procure them for their stables. But in 1499 King Charles expelled all Gypsies from Spain, under penalty of enslavement. King Philip III again ordered all Gypsies (Gitanos) out of Spain in 1619, this time under penalty of death. An exception was granted for those who would settle down in one place, dress as Spaniards, and stop speaking their ancient language. Philip IV lowered the penalties to six years on the galleys for men and a good flogging for women.

The King of France, Charles IX, banned Gypsies in 1561; he ordered that any Gypsy man caught in France to be sentenced to three years on the galleys, in spite of the fact that they were pronounced a non-violent people. In 1607, Henry IV enjoyed Gypsy dancers at court, but by 1666, Gypsy men were again condemned to galleys, this time for life, and Gypsy women caught in France had their heads shaved.

CHAPTER TWO

My name is Antony "Tony" Marshall, I am a true blooded Romany Gypsy, and my ancestry goes back hundreds of years in the UK. My blood line is of the Marshall/ Buckland/ Stanley/ Watson/ O'Neil/ McLean/ Campbell/ Penfold/ Smith and Broadway families; anyone who knows about Gypsy heritage will recognize these names as being old Romany family names with great historical values. This book tells some of the accounts of my ancestors and family members past and present.

Gypsies of late have unfairly been given a bad reputation due to the influx of non-Romany Gypsies coming into our country, with their way of life causing great concern for the everyday person as well as among our people. It was not so many years ago: our people were held in the highest regard, by gentry and farmers alike, for our services to their industries. I can remember my father telling us children tales of his childhood, of pulling into villages with wagons and horses and the local farmer begging my grandfather to stop on his farm to help with any repairs that may have been needed, or bringing in or harvesting of crops. Works such as tin masonry – hence the name tinkers – the making of horn spoons and utensils, basket weaving, broom and pegs, also fruit and hop picking, were known as traditional Gypsy work.

He would tell us of how he and my grandmother would hop off the wagon about a mile away from reaching the Hatching Tan (camping site) and walk the rest of the way, stopping off to hawk the local farmer's wives, selling them a lace tablecloth or telling their fortunes, and by the time they reached the camp would have a basket full of food – eggs, cheese, milk, bacon and if they were lucky a chicken for tea – they had taken as payments along the way. By this time my grandfather had set up camp, with the horse staked out and the chitty irons and pan on the fire ready to go. THE GOOD OLD DAYS.

CHAPTER THREE

The MARSHALLS:

The name Marshall originates from the French word *maréchal* meaning "horse servant". It was introduced into Britain following the Norman Conquest. The earliest record of the name is Maledoni Marechal who witnessed a gift of land in 1136: this would indicate that the bearer of the name was a responsible person who could read and write (in an age when illiteracy was the norm).

By 1296 the name had moved on to Marschal. There are records that a number of Marschals as landed gentry were amongst those required by King Edward 1 of England to pay homage and sign the Ragman Roll.

This story begins with my great-great-grandfather William "King Billy" Marshall, a legend of a man.

KING BILLY:

William "Billy" Marshall was born in 1672 in the county of Ayrshire, which is in the southwest of Scotland, the county seat being the city of Ayr. He is buried in St Cuthbert's churchyard in Kirkcudbright (pronounced Kirr-Koo-Bree), a town in the south of Scotland in Dumfries and Galloway. The town lies south of Castle Douglas and Dalbeattie, in an area known as the Stewartry, situated at the mouth of the river Dee some six miles from the sea.

Billy Marshall lived until 1792 making him 120 years old, and was known to be the King of the Gypsies. He was also known as the "Caird of Burullion", *caird* meaning a skilled Gypsy, referring to ceardon (a skilled worker who practices some trade or handicraft). Barullion is the name of a range of hills in the county of Wigtonshire in the council area of Dumfries-Galloway, in southern Scotland. Another so-called title of his was "King of the Randies". The word *randies* in this context refers to a type of macho man that despised all rule and authority. He was a Gypsy descendant of Roma people, and the embodiment of an 18th century Galloway Pict. When it came to fighting the Picts were some of the fiercest and highly organized warriors of Britain in Roman times, and were never conquered by the Romans.

King Billy was a boxer before the establishment of classic boxing rules in the mid-1800's. It was bare-knuckle boxing with no rules that allowed eye gouging, hair pulling, head butting, chin kicks, and wrestling. There may have been three bouts, with each bout being of a different sort of fighting; one bout would have been with bare fists, another with sword and knives and a third with cudgels or quarterstaffs (long sticks). King Billy was well known and renowned in this fighting circle as a ferocious warrior of a man who fought without fear and remorse for his victories, as victory in this sport often ended with the death of your opponent. King Billy fought as a soldier in the army and navy of King William III at the Battle of Boyne. He had deserted the army seven times and the navy three, had also served within some of the British regiments under the great Duke of Marlborough in Germany, about the year 1705. But at this period King Billy's military career in the service of his country ended. He went to his commanding officer informing him that he was going to Keltonhill Fair (old Gypsy horse fair) as he had made it a rule never to be absent, for it was at these occasions that challenges would be made to his claim to be the best fighting man among Gypsies. His commanding officer is recorded as later saying, "I thought it needless to take any very strong measure to hinder him" (don't blame him) and King Billy was at Keltonhill Fair accordingly.

His military experience may have helped him to organize his people into gangs in the Barullion hills. Him and his Gypsy band called "the Levelers" would tear down walls and dykes that landed gentry built to route water away from the peasant farms; his "Levelers" would also tear down the King's fences, allowing cattle to roam freely. King Billy also owned a public house which was renowned amongst Gypsies and Gorgers (non-Gypsies) alike as a safe haven for those on the run from the law or establishment.

King Billy was a renowned judge of horse and cattle, and was known to be called upon from people of high distinction to aid in the acquiring of such. This is a trait that runs throughout the history of the Gypsy race to this day, as some of the finest bred horses of modern age originate from this breed.

King Billy served and fought for his country as thousands of Gypsies have over the centuries. Gypsy men have taken part in every war our country has played part in, losing their lives in the hope of keeping our homeland safe, yet there are no tributes, no statues or monuments to the fallen men of the Gypsy people who paid the ultimate price in the defense of this land, "our Land".

Every cavalry that has ever fought for this country, a Gypsy man would have had a hand in the acquiring and trading of the horses, for this purpose, for when it comes to the judging of grys (horses) the Gypsy is second to none. There are not many Gypsies with documented ancestry such as I: the fact that King Billy can be looked up on Google or Wikipedia, bearing in mind he was a Gypsy man, is no mean feat.

CHAPTER FOUR

In accounts of King Billy, he is said to have been married 17 times and fathered over 100 children, two after the age of 100. This I believe to be untrue, for we are a small breed of people. The tale goes that this came about when strangers would enter his encampment asking who the women were and if they were married or not, they would be told they were all his wives and the children were all his, therefore stopping any untoward advances that may have been made.

What follows is an account of one gentleman from an article in *Blackwood's Edinburgh Magazine* from 1817 telling of a meeting with King Billy.

This item was a letter to the editor of Blackwood's Edinburgh Magazine April - September 1817.

SOME ACCOUNT OF BILLY MARSHAL, A GYPSEY CHIEF.

AMONG some instructive and many very entertaining articles in your Magazine, I have been a good deal amused in reading your account of the gypsies, and more particularly of the gypsies of our own country. The race has certainly degenerated (if I may be allowed to use the expression), and is in some risk of becoming extinct, whether to the advantage of society or not I will leave to the profound to determine. In the mean time, I am very well pleased that you have united with the anonymous author of Guy Mannering, in recording the existence, the manners, and the customs, of this wonderful people.

But, I have been, I assure you, in no small degree disappointed, when reading the names of the Faas, the Baileys, the Gordons, the Shaws, the Browns, the Keiths, the Kennedys, the Ruthvens, the Youngs, the Taits, the Douglasses, the Blythes, the Allans, and the Montgomeries, &c. — to observe so noted a family as the Marshals altogether omitted. I beg leave to add, that your author will be considered either a very ignorant, or a very partial historian, by all the readers and critics in the extensive districts of Galloway and Ayrshire, if he persists in passing over in silence the distinguished family of Billy Marshal, and its numerous cadets. I cannot say that I, as an individual, owe any obligations to the late Billy Marshal; but, sir, I am one of an old family in the Stewartry of Galloway, with whom Billy was intimate for nearly a whole century. He visited regularly, twice a year, my great-grandfather, grandfather, and father, and partook, I dare say, of their hospitality; but he made a grateful and ample return ; for during all the days of Billy's natural life, which the sequel will shew not to have been few, the washings could have been safely left out all night, without any thing, from a sheet or a tablecloth down to a dishclout, being in any danger. During that long period of time, there never was a goose, turkey, duck, or hen, taken away, but what could have been clearly traced to the fox, the brock, or the fumart; and I have heard an old female domestic of ours declare, that she had known Billy Marshal and his gang, again and again, mend all the "kettles, pans, and crackit pigs, in the house, and mak twa or three dozen o' horn spoons into the bargain, and never tak a farthing o' the laird's siller."

I am sorry that I cannot give you any very minute history of my hero: however, I think it a duty I owe on account of my family, not to allow, as far as I can hinder it, the memory, and name, of so old a friend and benefactor to fall into oblivion, when such people as the Faas and Baileys, &c. are spoken of.

Where he was born I cannot tell. Who were his descendants I cannot tell; I am sure he could not do it himself, if he were living. It is known that they were prodigiously numerous; I dare say, numberless. For a great part of his long life, he reigned with sovereign sway over a numerous and powerful gang of gypsey tinkers, who took their range over Carrick in Ayrshire, the Carrick mountains, and over the Stewartry and Shire of Galloway ; and now and then, by way of improving themselves, and seeing more of the world, they crossed at Donaghadee, and visited the counties of Down and Derry. I am not very sure about giving you up Meg Merrilies quite so easily; I have reason to think, she was a Marshal, and not a Gordon: and we folks in Galloway think this attempt of the Borderers, to rob us of Meg Merrilies, no proof that they have become quite so religious and pions, as your author would have us to believe, but rather that, with their religion and piety, they still retain some of their ancient habits. We think this attempt to deprive us of Meg Merrilies almost as bad as that of the descendants of the barbarous Picts, now inhabiting the banks of the Dee in Aberdeenshire, who some years ago attempted to run off with the beautiful lyric of Mary's Dream; and which we were under the necessity of proving, in one of the courts of Apollo, to be the effusion of Low's muse, on the classic and romantic spot, situated at the conflux of the Dee and the Ken, in the Stewartry of Galloway. But to return from this digression to Billy Marshal: - I will tell you everything more about him I know ; hoping this may catch the eye of someone who knew him better, and who will tell you more.

Billy Marshal's account of himself was this: he was born in or about the year 1666; but he might have been mistaken as to the exact year of his birth; however, the fact never was doubted, of his having been a private soldier in the army of King William, at the battle of the Boyne. It was also well known, that he was a private in some of the British regiments, which served under the great Duke of Marlborough in Germany, about the year 1705. But at this period, Billy's military career in the service of his country ended. About this time he went to his commanding officer, one of the McGuffogs of Ruscoe, a very old family in Galloway, and asked him if he had any commands for his native country: being asked if there was any opportunity, he replied, yes; he was going to Keltonhill fair, having for some years made it a rule never to be absent. His officer knowing his man, thought it needless to take any very strong measure to hinder him; and Billy was at Keltonhill accordingly.

Now Billy's destinies placed him in a high sphere; it was about this period, that, either electively, or by usurpation, he was placed at the head of that mighty people in the south west, whom he governed with equal prudence and talent for the long space of eighty or ninety years. Some of his admirers assert, that he was of royal ancestry, and that he succeeded by the laws of hereditary succession ; but no regular annals of Billy's house were kept, and oral tradition and testimony weigh heavily against this assertion. From any research I have been able to make, I am strongly disposed to think, that, in this crisis of his life, Billy Marshal had been no better than Julius Caesar, Richard III., Oliver Cromwell, Hyder Ally, or Napoleon Bonaparte: I do not mean to say, that he waded through as much blood as some of those, to seat himself on a throne, or to grasp at the diadem and sceptre; but it was shrewdly suspected, that Billy Marshal had stained his character and his hands with human blood. His predecessor died very suddenly, it never was supposed by his own hand, and he was buried as privately about the foot of Cairnsmuir, Craig Nelder, or the Corse of Slakes, without the ceremony, or, perhaps more properly speaking, the benefit of a precognition being taken, or an inquest held by a coroner's jury. During this long reign, he and his followers were not outdone in their exploits, by any of the colonies of Kirk-Yetholm, Horncliff, Spital, or Lochmaben. The following anecdote will convey a pretty correct notion, of what kind of personage Billy was, in the evening of his life; as for his early days, I really know nothing more of them than what I have already told.

The writer of this, in the month of May 1789, hail returned to Galloway after a long absence: he soon learned that Billy Marshal, of whom he had heard so many tales in his childhood, was still in existence. Upon one occasion he went to Newton-Stewart, with the late Mr M'Culloch of Barholm and the late Mr Hannay of Bargaly, to dine with Mr Samuel M'Caul. Billy Marshal then lived at the hamlet or clachan of Polnure, a spot beautifully situated on the burn or stream of that name; we called on our old hero, - he was at home, — he never denied himself, — and soon appeared; — he walked slowly, but firmly towards the carriage, and asked Mr Hannay, who was a warm friend of his, how he was? — Mr Hannay asked if he knew who was in the carriage? he answered, that his eyes " had failed him a gude dale;" but, added, that he saw his friend Barholm, and that he could see a youth sitting betwixt them, whom he did not know. I was introduced, and had a gracious shake of his hand. He told me I was setting out in life, and admonished me to "tak care o my han', and do naething to dishonor the gude stock o' folk that I was come o';" he added, that I was the fourth generation of us he had been acquaint wi'. Each of us paid a small pecuniary tribute of respect, — I attempted to add to mine, but Barholm told me, he had fully as much as would be put to a good use.

We were returning the same way, betwixt ten and eleven at night, after spending a pleasant day, and taking a cheerful glass with our friend Mr M'Caul; we were descending the beautifully wooded hills, above the picturesque glen of Polnure, — my two companions were napping, — the moon shone clear, — and all nature was quiet, excepting Polnure burn, and the dwelling of Billy Marshal, — the postilion stopt (in these parts the well-known, and well-liked Johnny Whurk), and turning round with a voice which indicated terror he said, "Gude guide us, there's folk singing psalms in the wud.'" My companions awoke and listened, — Barholm said, "psalms, sure enough;" but Bargaly said, " the deil a-bit o' them are psalms." We went on, and stopt again at the door of the old king: we then heard Billy go through a great many stanzas of a song, in such a way that convinced us that his memory and voice, had, at any rate, not failed him; he was joined by a numerous and powerful chorus. It is quite needless to be so minute as to give any account of the song which Billy sung; it will be enough to say that my friend Barholm was completely wrong, in supposing it to be a psalm; it resembled in no particular, psalm, paraphrase, or hymn. We called him out again, — he appeared much brisker than he was in the morning: we advised him to go to bed; but he replied, that "he didna think he wad be muckle in his bed that night, — they had to tak the country in the morning (meaning, that they were to begin a ramble over the country), and that they "were just takin a wee drap drink to the health of our honours, wi' the lock siller we had gi'en them." I shook hands with him for the last time, — he then called himself above one hundred and twenty years of age: he died about 1790.

His great age never was disputed to the extent of more than three or four years. The oldest people in the country allowed the account to be correct - The great-grandmother of the writer of this article died at the advanced age of one hundred and four; her age was correctly known. She said, that Wull Marshal was a man when she was a bitt callant, (provincially, in Galloway, a very young girl.) She had no doubt as to his being fifteen or sixteen years older than herself, and he survived her several years. His long reign, if not glorious, was in the main fortunate for himself and his people. Only one great calamity befel him and them, during that long space of time in which he held the reins of government. It may have been already suspected, that with Billy Marshal ambition was a ruling passion; and this bane of human fortune had stimulated in him a desire to extend his dominions from the Brigg end of Dumfries to the Newton of Ayr, at a time when he well knew the braes of Glen-Nap, and the Water of Doon, to be his western precinct. He reached the Newton of Ayr, which I believe is in Kyle; but there he was opposed, and compelled to re-cross the river, by a powerful body of tinkers from Argyle or Dumbarton. He said, in his bulletins, that they were supported by strong bodies of Irish sailors, and Kyle colliers. Billy had no artillery, but his cavalry and infantry suffered very severely. He was obliged to leave a great part of his baggage provisions, and camp equipage, behind him ; consisting of kettles, pots, pans, blankets, crockery, horns, pigs, poultry, &c. A large proportion of shelties, asses, and mules, were driven into the water and drowned, which occasioned a heavy loss, in creels, panniers, hampers, tinkers' tools, and cooking utensils; and although he was as well appointed, as to a medical staff, as such expeditions usually were, in addition to those who were missing, many died of their wounds. However, on reaching Maybole with his broken and dispirited troops, he was joined by a faithful ally from the county of Down; who, unlike other allies on such occasions, did not forsake him in his adversity. This junction enabled our hero to rally, and pursue in his turn: a pitched battle was again fought, somewhere about the Brigg of Doon or Alloway Kirk; when both sides, as is usual, claimed a victory; but, however this may have been, it is believed that this disaster, which happened A. D. 1712, had slaked the thirst of Billy's ambition: He was many years in recovering from the effects of this great political error; indeed, it had nearly proved as fatal to the fortunes of Billy Marshal, as the ever memorable Russian campaign did to Napoleon Bonaparte, about the same year in the succeeding century.

It is usual for writers, to give the character along with the death of their prince or hero: I would like to be excused from the performance of any such task, as drawing the character of Billy Marshall; but it may be done in a few words, by saying, that he had from nature a strong mind, with a vigorous and active person; and that, either naturally or by acquirement, he possessed every mental and personal quality, which was requisite for one who was placed in his high station, and who held sovereign power over his fellow-creatures for so great a length of time.

CHAPTER FIVE

King Billy did have many children, one of whom was my great-grandfather Billy Marshall (aka Bulla). It is not known where or when he was born as records of Gypsy births in this day and age did not exist.

I have been told stories of my great-grandfather that he again was a powerhouse of a man who followed in King Billy's footsteps as a boxer (fighting man), taking up the mantle of best man among the Gypsies of his time. The name Bulla was given as a reference to him being a bull of a man, as these men were giants of this age, standing at over six feet tall when the average was five feet seven.

Boxing was and is to this day a tradition amongst Gypsies handed down from generation to generation as the sport of choice and also as a means of self-defense, producing some of the finest boxers of modern times with many going on to become champions of the world, great fighters like Jem Mace of olden times; Mathew Hilton of Canada who held and defended the IBF belt several times; Gypsy Johnny Frankham who held the British Light Heavyweight title; and of modern times Gypsy Billy Joe Saunders who represented the United Kingdom at the Olympics, turned pro and now holds the British and Commonwealth belts; also Gypsy Tyson Fury who I believe will one day be Heavyweight Champion of the World; Tyson is married to my sister Linda's girl Paris. This is to name but a few; there have been and will be many more, as for the reason, if you attend any boxing club in the world, there will be Gypsies training there and representing that club at the highest level.

It is not just in boxing that Gypsies have excelled but in so many sports like football, with the likes of Eric Cantona of France probably the best Man United player of modern times, Zlatan Ibrahimavic of Sweden, Andrea Pirlo of Italy, Ricardo Quaresma of Portugal, Rafael Van Der Varrt of Holland, Jesus Navas of Spain, and Christo Stoickov, to name but a few. If the Gypsy football players of Europe were to form a team its starting eleven could win the World Cup. Also in the fields of acting, stars such as Sir Charles Chaplin, Sir Michael Caine, Yul Brynner, Bob Hoskins, Rita Hayworth, and in music the likes of Ronnie Wood of the Rolling

Stones, David Essex, Johnny Cash (who admitted to being of Romany descent is his last autobiography), and even the great Elvis Presley whose mother was a Smith and his father was of German Senti Romany stock. In the art world there was Pablo Picasso. Even Mother Teresa admitted to being half-Gypsy, and here's one that I don't think many people know about. Bill Clinton, yes the ex-President of the United States of America, one-time most powerful man on earth, is of Romany stock, and while in office drafted into effect laws that would give the Gypsies of America a better way of life.

Slowly but surely Gypsies are becoming more open of their heritage as in the past we were more guarded and secretive of this for fear of rejection or non-inclusion. I feel that non-Gypsies' perspectives and fear of the unknown about Gypsies are becoming less and less, due in part to television programs such as *My Big Fat Gypsy Wedding*, that have shown another side to Travelers, with even the Irish Traveler Paddy Doherty winning *Celebrity Big Brother*, although these programs are in general about Irish Travelers. To Gorgers (non-Gypsies) we are all classed the same, so any good publicity can't hurt. Times are changing and only for the better. Now back to my story.

Why my great-grandfather did not take up the official title of King of the Gypsies is not known, as being the eldest son of King Billy it would have been his right. It is thought that he preferred to live more of a quiet life and traveled freely throughout the border regions of the UK, settling in a border town called Newton Stewart; he was married to a woman called Katy O'Neil, and had four children. My great-grandmother Katy's family is one of the oldest traditional Gypsy families, their name goes back in history as long as any other and can still be found today throughout the world.

My grandfather Joseph Marshall was born in their wagon as were all of the children, him being the second oldest of four. His elder brother Billy ("the Gurkha") carrying on the traditional first name. Billy was nicknamed "the Gurkha" because of the darkness of his skin and his prowess with a knife. The tales of these two brothers as young men are legendary, for their skills both as fighters and amazing judges of horse. It is said that if they attended a fair (Gypsy meeting place) other Gypsy men would flock around them to listen to their accounts, and Gypsy women would flock around them for their handsome good looks. They were less than a year apart in age yet completely deferent in looks, Billy being as black as coal and my grandfather being blond-haired and blue-eyed. Billy was said to be the shorter of the two but powerfully built, with Joe standing at over six feet tall. They were very widely traveled for this age, attending fairs throughout the country ranging from Bucky in the north of Scotland to Appleby and Stow in the south of England. This was an unbelievable journey in these times when you take into account they were traveling with horse and wagon.

While attending a horse fair in Newcastle upon Tyne my grandfather met my grandmother Agnes McLean, the daughter of another legendary fighting man of the north of England, Johnny McLean. She was the third youngest of four children and was said to be beautiful beyond belief. The McLeans are again one of the oldest Gypsy families known in the UK. Famous for their tents and wagons, they were renowned for their close family ties, and their resemblance to American Indians. It is known they would have one large communal tent, where all the family would congregate for meetings and meals, with smaller living tents for sleeping. These tents were shaped like teepees, therefore leading to the comparison to Indians.

My grandmother had two older sisters and one younger brother, Johnny McLean Jr, who against his father's wishes went with most of the young men of the family to join the army and fight in the First World War, losing his life to the bullet of a sniper rifle. The story is that two days before the end of the war, while sitting in a trench with other members of Gypsy soldiers, he accepted a cigarette from his cousin and as it was lit a sniper shot him in the head, killing him instantly. The tragedy of this tale was still to unfold for not only did this brave young man lose his life, his father and mother who had not left the land they were staying on when he left, for fear that on his return he would not know where to find them, did not know of his death, and on hearing the news that the war had ended were rejoicing along with the other members of the family, thinking their only son would soon be returning, A week later while busying themselves in the cleaning up of the site in preparation of a homecoming party, my great-grandfather Johnny was cutting the grass around the wagon with a scythe, when up pulled the local policeman on a pedal-bike. This policeman was known to the family as they had lived in this area for some time, and he was known to have a hatred for the Gypsy race.

After asking to speak with my great-grandfather – what follows is a true account of events – the police officer asked, "Are you Johnny McLean?"

"Yes," replied my great-grandfather.

"Do you have a son called Johnny?"

"Yes," replied my great-grandfather.

"Well not anymore," said the officer, "as he has been killed in action and won't be coming home."

This, as the story goes, was said in such a nonchalant way from the officer as though he was talking about a stray dog. At that moment my great-grandfather instantly lost his mind, attacking the bearer of this news. Still holding the scythe he was using to cut the grass, he was said to have cut the officer's arm completely off from the elbow with one swipe. If not for the actions of his family in stopping him I believe he would have killed this person, for delivering this tragic news of the loss of his only son and namesake in such a heartless manner. My great-grandfather was arrested for the attempted murder of the officer and sentenced to life in prison. He never recovered from this loss, and is said to have lost his mind on that day. He died in a prison for the criminally insane.

CHAPTER SIX

My grandfather Joe and grandmother Agnes were married in Newcastle and returned to the Galloway borders, giving birth to three children, Elithebeth (Betty) the eldest, William (Dids) and then some fourteen years later my father, Johnny McLean Marshall, named after my great-grandfather. My grandmother was said to have lost many children in between Dids and my father. As you can imagine being in labor in those days was no easy task, in most cases the baby being born with only the aid of the older female members in attendance, in a tent, or if you were very fortunate a wagon.

They traveled throughout this region, and my father used to hold us transfixed with his tales of these days, accounts of his childhood stopping places and where they would make for in the winters, stories of him and some of his oldest friends rambling about, coursing with dogs, guddling (fishing by hand) for fish, bringing home their catches for the women to cook. As a child I would listen to these tales, thinking how wonderful this sounded, but in reality these were hard times, but they made the best of what they had or in most cases didn't have, and enjoyed life to the full, moving from one stopping place to the next, always welcomed by the locals. With the women keeping the table and the men trading in horses and wagons this was a very hand to mouth existence, but if you listen to the Gypsy people of these times, they were happy times. My father told us of his older brother who was his childhood hero, tales of his fights – one of which is legendary in the north of England, between him and the so-called Best Man amongst Gypsies (the "Black Cat").

When this man declared himself to be the Best Man on the fair my uncle Dids took affront to this, and said, "How can you be the Best Man on this fair when you have not beaten me?", and so the fight was on. Both men were in their prime at the age of twenty-one and of similar build, giants of this time with the two of them standing at over 6 feet 3 inches, powerful, highly trained fighting machines: it is said they fought for over half an hour, with my uncle knocking him out, stopping the fight. This man's father came running with a kettle prop to hit my uncle from behind, only to run straight onto a right hand from my grandfather, knocking him out alongside his son.

CHAPTER SEVEN

My Father Johnny McLean Marshall was born in Kilmarnock in Ayeshire in 1927, being the youngest of three children. His mother died at a very young age when my father was only 11 years old. His father Joe turned to drink, more so to try and drown out the guilt he felt for the loss of his wife, for he was known to be a spiteful man to her in his day. One of my earliest memories is going to visit him in a little cottage in Kilmarnock, and him giving me a football. I could have only been three years of age. The next memory of him is in the hospital on his deathbed. My mother, father and I went to see him and he did not know who we were, until my father gave him a little shot of whiskey against the orders of the nurses; but once he had a drink he picked right up and was sitting up in bed speaking to us of old times, asking if I still had the football he had given me. He died shortly after and I, my mother and younger sister attended his funeral. My father could not attend as he was wanted by the police at the time.

My father was as you would expect a bit of a tearaway after the loss of his mother who was the light of his life as he was hers. With his father taking to the drink he was left to his own devices, free to roam at will. His sister Betty was 17 years his elder and after marrying at sixteen had children the same age as him. He would spend time both with his sister and brother Billy, nicknamed "Dids" for the reason of when he was a little boy if asked if he had done something wrong he would reply "I dids not do it", so Dids; and it stuck with him throughout his life. My father would tell us stories of this time, how the loss of his mother had a very deep effect on him, and the feeling of being unwanted by the rest of his family, with his brother and sister having children of their own (Nan the same age), he felt that they thought of him as a bit of a bad influence on their own kids, so he was shuttled from one to the other. By the age of thirteen he had started going off the rails and getting into trouble with the law for stealing, so he was sent to live with his brother full-time. By the age of sixteen he had become a full-time criminal, with burglary of industrial factories being his target. What you have to remember is that these were the hardest of times and people of no or very little education were struggling to survive, and throughout his life my father wanted more from life than just to survive.

By sixteen he had been sentenced to borstal for his wrongdoings, and during this time inside was to meet one of his oldest friends, Jimmy Divit. My father had from childhood attended the boxing clubs in and about Edinburgh and Glasgow, and by his teenage years was a well-rounded boxer with skills above his tender years. Jimmy Divit was an amateur boxing champion who like my father had gone off the rails and found himself in borstal for some petty crime or other and had the run of the establishment ("The Daddy") being nearly eighteen and the head of the borstal boxing team; it would have taken a very good young fighter to knock him off his perch. Upon entry to the borstal my father was inducted into the boxing team as they knew of him from his bouts in the local area. Jimmy Divit was friendly to my father but was wary of him, I suppose wondering if he had thoughts of becoming "The Daddy" himself, so rather than tackle my father head on devised a plan to see just how good my father was, having his second in command offend my father to see how he would react. My father said this young man and him got to arguing and agreed to have a straightener (fair fight) the next day, so as not to get re-arrested or be sentenced to more time. During lunch break if you had a row the screws (prison guards) would allow the two of you to go into a storeroom to sort out your differences man to man, with who walks out the winner.

My father told us boys many times of how this young man could fight, telling how he hit him with good shots only for him to fight back like a lion. But the young man had a bad habit of ducking down out of the way of the right hand. My father taking mental note of this feigned with the right and when he ducked, kicked him as hard as he could, knocking him spark out. Leaving the room he was greeted by looks of amazement from the other prisoners as he was the much smaller of the two and this young man had such a fearsome reputation as a fighter. After regaining consciousness my father's opponent came and shook his hand, telling all who would listen how good of a fighter my father was, saying that when he ducked my father hit him with the hardest uppercut he had ever felt. It had happened so quickly, he had thought my father had hit him with his hand not his foot. Needless to say my father never corrected him and the tale did his own reputation no harm at all.

After this Jimmy and my father became firm friends, going on to box successfully for the borstal on numerous occasions. Jimmy Divit went on to be one of the hardest and most notorious of Edinburgh gangsters, He was found dead in the Haymarket in Edinburgh with an army bayonet so far embedded into his back that it was sticking out of his chest.

CHAPTER EIGHT

Upon his release from borstal after serving nearly two years, my father was drafted into the army but after his mother had told him as a child time and time again of how her brother had lost his life and made him promise her he would never go to war, he made up his mind he would keep his word to her, so he came up with the plan of action that he would not follow any orders and even more so if anyone gave him an order he would lay into (hit) them. This it seemed was doing the trick, or so he thought. After one encounter with a drill sergeant he was taken to the stockade, then on to Edinburgh Castle which was being used at that time as a military prison.

Every morning my father and the rest of the prisoners would be taken from their cells into an exercise yard for to wash and walk around. My father had noticed that next to the sink was a large roll of towel like the ones used to fill the towel machines in public toilets. Picking a moment when the guards were distracted he grabbed the towel roll and threw it over the top of the wall so as it caught on the barbed wire.

Using this as a rope he climbed up to the top of the wall. Upon reaching the top, with the guards shouting for him to get down or they would shoot, he peered over the other side. Seeing a sheet of what he thought to be mist on the ground about twenty feet below, and deciding there was no going back, he jumped, going straight through what he now realized was fog and the twenty feet he had to jump became more like seventy. My father has taken us so many times when we were in Edinburgh to show us the exact spot he jumped from, and as anyone who knows the Castle will testify, the back side is a wall of over 60 feet with a hill below that's too steep to climb of about 200 feet. My father said it felt as though he was falling for an eternity before hitting the ground and tumbling down the hill hitting an iron fence at the bottom. We used to look in awe as he would tell us of how he escaped from Edinburgh Castle.

It was not very long after that the military police caught up with him, sending him to a military prison. Carrying on with his master plan of attacking everyone who gave him an order ended with him being sent to a Military hospital for evaluation. Thinking he had cracked it and after a bit more play-acting he would be expelled from the army, but this was going to be more difficult than he ever dreamed. My father said this was by far the worst place he had ever seen, full of people who had truly lost their minds. He told us of how one day looking out of the hatch on his door he saw another young Gypsy man he knew staring at him from the cell opposite his. Thinking to himself, "Good, at last I have a bit of company", he shouted out to this boy to come speak with him, but no reply. Again he shouted, "You know who I am brother, gel akie and rocker to mandy (come here and talk with me)."

Again no reply, and then this boy popped his head out of the hatch and said, "Want to see what I've got?"

Before my father could answer he put his hand out of the hatch and opened it to reveal every one of his teeth: he had pulled them all out by hand. My father asked him why he had done this, only once again to be greeted by silence. After this my father said all he wanted to do was get out of this place and set about trying to convince the doctors of his sanity, but it is one thing putting on an act of being divvy (crazy) but a whole other matter trying to convince them you are not, and after spending several long months in this ungodly place he was released and excused from the army, with the diagnosis of being a manic depressive schizophrenic.

CHAPTER NINE

My father again went to live with his brother Dids, his wife Dinah and two children Beverly and Lee, who at this time were living in Manchester as this was where Dinah came from, being of a local traveling family called Waters. He took up with Dinah's sister, called Silvia, and went on to have two children with her, Lavern and Johnny.

He was still a bit of a rogue and had never stopped with his life of crime. Working in partnership with his brother and several other members of their gang they targeted railway storage yards. Remember, this was just after the war and everything was rationed, there was still American soldiers stationed throughout the UK who received far better supplies then our soldiers could ever dream of, from chocolate bars to chewing gum, soap, shampoos, even down to stockings that would be handed out as gifts for the local young ladies, these being a luxury that only the richest of people could afford at this time, so on the black market sold in no time for great profit. This was a very good business for my father and his brother, but as the saying goes "all good things must come to an end". This one was about to with a bump.

It was on a freezing cold winters night. My father, Dids and the gang was coming out of a railway depot in the north of England in the early hours of the morning after unloading a carriage of its goods, my uncle Dids driving their vehicle and the boys behind in the loaded lorry, when out of nowhere stepped a police officer into the middle of the road. This was long before the use of radio walkie-talkies, and he had been riding a bike that now sat at the side of the road. Putting his hand up for them to stop, but this was not an option for the gang as they knew that if caught for the crime of stealing government goods they would all be going to prison for a very very long time, so my uncle put his toe down and went to drive around the officer, but to their surprise he came running at the car, pulling a whistle from his pocket and blowing it as loud as he could, I remember my father telling us of him thinking, "We are in the middle of nowhere who do you think is going to hear the whistle?"

By now the car was up to about 40 mile an hour, fast for the cars of that day, when thinking this officer would step aside and let them go by, to their surprise he jumped onto the bonnet of the car, shouting at them to pull over. They carried on driving with him holding on to the windscreen wipers, swerving from side to side in the hope he would fall off, but to no avail, my father and uncle shouting at him to get off and just let them go. In the end my uncle said, "Are you getting off?"

"No," came the reply from the policeman, "I will hold on till you have to stop, you're both under arrest."

Again not an option open to the occupants of this car, so turning around in the road my uncle Dids drove back into the railway yard and drove directly into a huge pile of coal used for the fueling of the steam locomotives. The police officer flew off of the front of the car and laid there motionless. By now the overnight guard who had been in on the robbery came running over, my uncle and father telling him, "Don't just stand there, go phone an ambulance" before they made their getaway.

This as you can imagine was front page news: "Robbery Gang Wanted for Attempted Murder of Police Officer". Time to gel (go). My father and uncle went to Ireland with the rest of the gang heading in other directions, but it was not long before the police came knocking at the door, due to someone giving up information as to their whereabouts. They were taken to Portlaoise Prison in County Laois in readiness for their return to the UK. They would both tell me tales of this time in later life, of how this prison was like something out of ancient history, a ruin of a place and of how even the guns the guards carried were old and rusty.

It was while in this prison they had their first encounter with Irish Travelers, with one of them being the top dog of the prison and wanting to try and demonstrate his authority among the other prisoners, by showing what he could do with the English hard men. My father and uncle had been put to work in the prison workshop sewing postal bags, when they were approached by this Irish Traveler. "You two," he said. "You will sew my bags," pointing to my father, "and you will sew my cousin's bags," pointing to my uncle Dids.

"I don't think so," replied my father.

"Oh I know so," said this man, reaching out to put his hand on my father's shoulder.

"Big Mistake". With one glance at each other my father and uncle knew what each other was thinking and as quick as a flash set into these two Travelers, as their motto was, as most fighting men will tell you even to this day, "Hit first and hit hard". My father and uncle had no trouble in disposing of the two would-be bullies but did not take into account that they were working in a shop full of the defeated men's families. A pitched battle broke out, with my father and uncle trading blows with an unknown amount of men. My father, breaking a chair and handing a leg to my uncle, proceeded to beat as many as they could but hugely outnumbered were getting as good as they were giving.

At that point the guards rushed in breaking up the battle, pointing their rifles at my father and uncle: "Stop or we will shoot you, English men." While being marched at gunpoint to the block (punishment cells) my father noticed that my uncle had been stabbed with a pair of industrial scissors right between the shoulder blades; in the heat of the fight with the adrenaline flowing he didn't even feel it. My uncle was taken to the hospital wing of the prison and my father put in the block, as they were due to be shipped back to Britain to stand trial for the attempted murder. The prison officials took no further action against them for the fight and allowed my father back into full circulation, but this time "on his own". My father and Dids had put about eight of them in hospital including the top dog but that still left a few who felt they had a score to settle. I remember my father saying how he knew that the first time he entered the exercise yard he would be in danger of losing his life, but the only options open to him were go out or have himself put on the numbers (segregation) along with the nonces or grasses, again not an option. So out he went and instead of waiting, walked right up to the Travelers, asking, "Which one of you stabbed my brother?"

At first no one answered. I suppose they were a bit in shock at the affront of this English Gypsy man confronting them in this manner. Then one stood up, declaring, "I fucking stabbed your brother, what do you want to do about it?"

"Well," my father said, "I thought you Irish Travelers were fair fighting men and are known for giving another man fair play."

"We are," replied this fella, "but only if the men we are fighting show the same respect."

"Well," my father said, "I will fight the best one amongst you, with one condition: this is the end of the argument, my brother is coming out of the hospital and won't be able to move his arm let alone fight anyone, so win lose or draw this sorts it out once and for all."

At that point one of the older members of this family stepped forward and said, "Son I have got to give it to you you're a game young man, and I will guarantee, you will get fair play here today," and "Who am I fighting?" said my father.

"Me," said the one who had admitted to stabbing my uncle. The older man went to the guards and informed them that the two men were to have a fair fight to put an end to the feud, and this was agreed, my father saying the guards seemed pleased to be about to see a good fight.

A circle was formed in the centre of the yard and in stepped my father and his opponent, my father said this man was strong but lacked in boxing skills and after putting him down a couple of times he gave my father best (conceded the fight). After his release from the hospital my uncle Dids and my father were kept in this prison for several months until their extradition back to Britain, and the Irish Travelers were true men to their word and never sought any form of revenge or retribution.

CHAPTER TEN

After returning to Britain the charges of attempted murder were dropped against my father for lack of evidence and he was released from prison, but the case carried on for my uncle Dids in the crown court.

At the start of the trial the police officer was brought into court in a wheelchair with a brace around his neck. After weeks of prosecution evidence finally it was my uncle's turn to give his account of events. Taking his position in the dock he faced the judge and gave him a Masonic sign for a brother in need of help, as my uncle Dids was at this time a high-level member of the Masons. Stopping the proceedings the judge asked to see the defendant in his chambers. Upon entering the judge's room my uncle was asked questions of a secret nature confirming his rank and status within the Masonic lodge; once done they spoke freely. By the end of their meeting the judge said, "You have asked for my assistance and as an active member of the lodge and brother I cannot refuse your plea, but from this day forward you will no longer be a welcome member of yours or any other lodge."

Accepting this deal my uncle retook his place in the dock and at the end of the trial he was sentenced to 18 months in prison and released for time served. The police and the prosecution were up in arms at the leniency of the sentence, including the officer involved in the offence, who on hearing the verdict jumped from his wheelchair shouting abuse at my uncle and throwing his neck brace at him.

My uncle was blackballed from the Masons and never set foot in a Masonic lodge again. Many years later my father attempted to get him to come to a meeting, saying, "Come on that will all be forgotten now."

"No," replied my uncle, "I had my deal with the judge and I will stick with it."

On my father's release from prison he went back to Manchester and tried to carry on with life as normal with Silvia and the children, but the time away had made them distant and with rumors of her being unfaithful during his time away, he left Manchester and traveled back to Scotland to his father's house in Kilmarnock in Ayrshire. It was here that he met my mother, Phoebe Mary Buckland. My mother's family originate from the southwest coast of England, the family name Buckland being one of the oldest known breed of Gypsies in the UK. My mother was one of the finest examples of traditional Gypsy women, with long-flowing black hair, dark eyes, and olive-colored skin; tall and elegant, standing nearly six feet tall.

My grandfather George Buckland came to settle in Scotland after meeting and marrying my grandmother Agnes Watson, again the name Watson being a very old and traditional Gypsy family name. My grandfather's people were very widely travelled not just in this country but in the USA where my great-great-grandfather Tenant Buckland and his wife, Tsar, first visited over two hundred years ago. They would travel by ship with their wagons and horses to New York from where they would travel the length and breadth of the country. Gypsies by nature are a nomadic race of people but the Bucklands took this to a whole other level, for in that day and age it was like going to the moon. There is an account of them in the *New York Times*, asking who and where this tribe of people has come from; who live in wagons upon the fields of Yonkers in the city of New York, with the men dealing in horses and the woman folk telling fortunes of the people who came to see them.

The story is that these Gypsy men were such excellent judge of horse they were given the job of procurement for the US cavalry. This family would travel back and forth between England and America as frequently as modern day Gypsy's travel around Europe. I have seen records of ship manifests for Tenant and his brothers coming and going from here to there and back mostly spending the summers in the UK and the winters in the US, making sure they never missed the fair at Epsom Downs, as this was the main meeting venue for Gypsies of the south of England, and a meeting place of many a Gypsy man and wife. It was at this fair my great-grandfather met his wife Phoebe Stanley. Once again, as any historian of Gypsy heritage will confirm, the name Stanley goes back generations in British history.

Tenant was famous for being one of the first Gypsy men to own a car. He had brought back from America one called an Overland, pulling onto Epsom Downs towing a Reading Wagon. They were known as the "posh Gypsies", for in this day if you owned a good tent and horse you were doing well. It was on one of their trips to Epsom that my great-grandfather Tom Buckland was born. Again records show of him traveling back to America as an infant and again at the age of eight years old. Members of the family were even booked on the Titanic for its fateful maiden voyage, only to turn up late and miss the loading time, but there were many Gypsies who did not turn up late and were on board the ship when it went down. Full families were lost that day, sent to a watery grave at the bottom of the sea.

CHAPTER ELEVEN

My great grandfather Tom Buckland returned from America with his family, as his children were getting of an age to get married and as per tradition they would marry someone of English heritage, they also brought back a cine camera projector that showed a silent movie, something that the average man/woman on the street had never seen.

This turned out to be a gold mine for them as they would travel about the country setting up in the town halls of the local villages and towns charging an admission fee of entry to watch the motion picture. People would come from miles around to marvel at the five-minute film, with on most occasions the Mayor of the next town coming along to ask them to please bring it to his town, and if there was any commission in it for him. This work took them from one end of England to the next, across to Ireland, from Ireland to Scotland where my grandfather met my grandmother Agnes Watson, whose family can be found to this day in and around the Midlothian region. As a young man I can recall visiting my mother's uncle Bob Watson at his home in Wishaw listening to his stories of how he remembered my grandfather and his family pulling onto the camp they were staying at and thinking, "Who are these people with their fancy cars and wagons?", telling us how when my grandfather married his sister her parents worried he would take her back to America and they would never see her again. But this was not to be the case for he settled down in Scotland and never set eyes on America again.

My mother was one of seven children, three boys and four girls, my mother being born in Hollywood in Belfast on one of their many visits to Ireland, eventually ending up in Kilmarnock. It was here at the tender age of fifteen she met and fell in love with my father, who was some four years her elder. My father was known as the local bad boy with tales of his exploits and prison sentences being common knowledge, her father and mother warning her to "Stay away from that young man, he's trouble"; but as so many young people do, it seems the more you try and keep them away from that person the more of an attraction they become. After a short courtship my father and mother ran away together, getting married in Gretna Green. It was during the time of Appleby Horse Fair and my father knowing his sister Betty and her husband Bob Kennedy were staying on the fair decided to go and pay them a visit. I remember my father telling the story of how they were not made to feel very welcome, with the words, "You can't stay with us as we have no room in our tents."

My father had very little money at this time and could have done with a little bit of help, but too proud to let them know this said, "Oh we are not staying we are going to pull on (move) to the fair tomorrow, and just wanted to see where we are going to pitch our tent."

With my mother wondering what the hell he was talking about they said their goodbyes and left. On the way back from Appleby to Carlisle there was a petrol station at the bottom of a hill they had stopped at on the way there. By now it was dark and getting to the top of the hill near the station my father stopped the car, telling my mother to give it five minutes then, without starting the engine or putting on the lights, let the handbrake off and let the car freewheel down the hill and into the door of the garage; my mother saying, "What if the door is not open?"

"It *will* be open," my father said, so five minutes later my mother did as my father said, letting off the handbrake. The car slowly started down the hill, but as she got close she could see that the huge shutter door was still shut, then all of a sudden open it came with my father waving her in. She drove straight into the garage before bringing the car to a halt. Once inside my father greeted her with a smile, and they set about robbing the place. This, as you have to remember, was just after the war and everything was on ration books including petrol. Entering the office they found a safe with the key hanging on a hook next to it. Opening it they found a large amount of cash and ration tokens for just about anything you could mention.

My father opened the door and with my mother steering pushed the car out of the garage and once they were a safe distance away jumped in and drove as fast as his old car would take them. Reaching Carlisle they stopped the night in a nice hotel and first thing the next morning went to the Bedford agents, trading their old car for a new van, then on to the Stead and Simpson tent dealers picking out the best tent they had to offer; from here to the local department store where they picked up everything they needed to fill the tent – bedding, lighting and such. I remember them telling us kids about the look on everyone's face when they came back to the fair with all the new tackle. And of how people who were not too pleased to see them the day before was acting as if they were a king and queen. My father would say about this in later years, "It's a wonder what a few quid in your pocket can do."

CHAPTER TWELVE

After leaving Appleby they went their own way, with my father still having his roving ways and a wandering eye for the ladies. He was the type of man to say he was going for a loaf of bread in the morning and return three days later, leaving my mother alone sometimes on a camp or sometimes in a farmer's field by herself. During one of his many trips my mother sent a telegram to her father asking him to come and get her, taking her back to their home. My father turning up some days later to get her, was told to get out and leave her where she is by my mother's parents; that she was too young to be living in this way as she was still only sixteen, and if he came back again they would have him locked up. My grandfather contacted the registrar's office in Gretna Green telling them of her real age and had the wedding annulled. My father went his own way leaving my mother behind heartbroken, for no matter what he did then or in the future she loved him with all of her heart.

Returning to his brother he took back up with the mother of his first children deciding to give it another try, but he was still in love with my mother, and after some time he came back to Kilmarnock and attended a local dance hall he knew my mother would be at, begging her to give him one more chance and that he was a changed man, that he would treat her like she deserved to be treated.

My mother, still being in love with him, said, "If I go with you where would we go?"

"We will go to America," he said, "and start a new life together away from all this."

They ran away again to start a new life that brought many good times and many hard times as well. Before they could go to America my father said, "We need to get some money together", and during an attempted robbery was arrested and sent to Barlinnie Prison in Glasgow, with my mother once again returning to her parents' home, only this time expecting their first child John, who was to die of pneumonia at the tender age of just one year. My mother still to this day carries a picture of him in her purse wherever she goes.

After this my father decided he had to get out of this prison by whatever means necessary and devised an escape plan. Bribing one of the screws he managed to get his hands on some hacksaw blades and each night would slowly cut away at the bars of his cell window. As my father was known within the prison system as an escape artist following the Edinburgh Castle incident he was issued with a prison uniform with stripes down the arms and legs and on entering his cell in the evening had to place it outside of his cell door. Once the bars were nearly cut through, he again bribed the prison works officer to leave a ladder outside of the prison workshop. On a visit with my mother he told her to bring him some clothes and place them in a bag beneath a large tree he could see from his cell window, because when he made the escape his uniform would be outside of his cell.

Finally he was ready: cutting through the last bit of the bars and removing them from the window he lowered himself out of the window and dropped some twenty feet to the floor, making his way to the ladder then up onto the top of the wall, pulling the ladder up and down to the other side before climbing down to freedom. I remember him telling us of how he came across a man walking his dog and the look on his face, as by now it had started to rain and there was my father in just his underpants and nothing else. "Good evening," said my father to him as he walked by, trying to act as thou this was nothing out of the ordinary. "Good evening," said the man and just carried on along his way.

Making his way to the tree my father searched about for the bag of clothes but to no avail. Just as he was about to give up he found them under a pile of leaves. Pulling on the suit and shoes my mother had left for him he made good his escape. At this time there was only one other successful escape ever made from Barlinnie Prison and I don't think there has been one since.

Later in life I was to come across an ex-lifer who had served his sentence in Barlinnie. On hearing my last name he asked, "You wouldn't be related to Johnny Marshall who escaped from prison would you?"

"Yes he's my father," I said.

"Your father is a legend in Barlinnie and still talked about to this day of how he managed to do it and get rid of the 'Old Devil' Mr Stewart." This was a notorious prison guard famous for his brutality to the prisoners in his care.

CHAPTER THIRTEEN

It was not long before my father was re-arrested. As you can imagine, escaping from one of the most secure prisons in the UK became big news and was to bring about one of the largest manhunts in Scottish history. Upon his arrest they brought him back, as they always do, to the prison he escaped from. This is to show the other prisoners who may have thoughts of their own escape that you will only be caught and returned to where you came from. As my father entered his wing he was greeted by cheers from the other prisoners, and looks of hatred from the screws, for this was a major cause of embarrassment to them. Being brought up in front of the prison board of governors who demanded to know who had given him assistance in his escaping – i.e. saw blades and ladders – my father said, "I can't tell you, for it involves one of your guards and my life would be in danger." This news of involvement of one of their officers as you can imagine made their ears prick up and brought them to the edge of their seats.

"We demand to know who was involved," they shouted to my father.

"I will tell you but on these conditions," my father said. "(1) No further charges are to be brought against me for the escape. (2) No loss of time served. (3) Removal from this prison. All to be agreed in writing and witnessed by my solicitor."

"No way," came the reply from one of the governors.

"Well that's up to you," said my father, "but if you want to know who is rotten among you that is my price."

"Maybe some time in the block might help you to re-consider your options Mr Marshall," my father saying, "If you put me in the block I promise you will never find out."

Sending him out of the room while they deliberated, after two hours they called him back in: "OK you have a deal, we will notify your solicitor to be here tomorrow morning to make the arrangements."

Next day having his deal agreed and in his solicitor's hand he was brought back up in front of the governors. "OK let's have it Marshall the name of the guard who assisted you in this escape."

Now my father was many things but a grass was not one of them, and the last thing he was going to do was tell on the screw who gave him the blades and left out the ladder, but the "Old Devil", Mr Stewart, was a whole different matter. "It was Mr Stewart."

"Mr Stewart the head guard?" said the governor.

"Yes," replied my father.

"Well I don't believe it," said the governor, "he has been with us for years. Why would he do such a thing?"

"For money that's why," my father said.

The governors sent for Mr Stewart immediately, having him come into the room to stand alongside my father. Telling him of what my father said he went ballistic shouting and making grabs for my father. "Tell them the truth you gyppo bastard," he said to my father,

"It is the truth," he replied.

On this evidence the "Old Devil" was suspended from duty never to return again. So not only was my father being rejoiced for his escape but he had gotten rid of one of the worst prison guards to ever walk the corridors of Barlinnie Prison.

After his release from this sentence and vowing never to return my father went back to my mother and the only business he knew, choring (stealing). It was after one more near-miss, with him being spotted, knowing the police would be coming, he thought enough is enough. Going to my mother's sister Agnes and her husband Tommy Nelson they asked if they could have their birth certificates to apply for passports in their names.

"Of course you can," said my uncle Tommy and Aunt Agnes, "we are never going to use them and the last thing we want is to see you go back to prison."

By now my mother had given birth to my oldest sister Linda, and wanted more than anything just to live a normal life, away from all the temptations of criminal activities my father was involved in, so once they had the passports they decided to go to Canada and boarded a plane to Toronto not knowing what the future held for them but knowing they had to make a break from the life they were leaving behind.

What they failed to take into account was it was winter. Within two days of landing a cold front brought snowdrifts ten feet high, literally bringing everything to a halt. My mother and father had rented an apartment as it was too cold to even think about going into a trailer (caravan). I remember them telling us kids it was so cold there were news flashes advising people to stay inside as the air was so cold it could damage your lungs to breathe it. Now after a few weeks of this, the bit of money they had was dwindling and my father's intention of getting out and taking some painting or tarmac work was out of the question because of all the snow. Even getting out of there was impossible as the airport and roads were closed down so he thought I will have to take a job. Getting the local newspaper he looked through the job section, but most of the jobs were menial or very low paid. Coming across one ad for an expert welder something my father had never done in his life, he decided to apply for it and went along for an interview, telling the manager of the factory that he had just came from Scotland where he worked in the ship building industry carrying out this type of work.

"You sound perfect for the position John," the manager said, "but before we take you on, we are going to need you to do some test welding for us with our senior welder," calling into the office a man who my father said looked like a lumberjack, "this man will take you for the test."

Now my father had never so much as held a welding rod let alone carried out welding work, so when asked by this guy what type of test weld did he want to start with, my father decided to come clean and tell him the truth.

"Brother," he said, "I have got to be honest with you, I have never welded anything in my life, but I have come here from England to try and start a new life, been snowed in and have a wife and baby girl to feed, I am a very hard worker and if you show me something once I can pick it up instantly."

This guy looked at my father and said, "So you're bullshitting."

"Yes but I really need this job."

"OK I will tell you what I am prepared to do, and I will give you half an hour of my time teaching you how to weld. After that if I think you ain't good enough I am telling the boss not to hire you, cos I need someone to help me get through all the work we have here and I ain't got no time for anyone who can't do their share."

My father said that after the half hour he was welding like he had been doing it for years, with the guy not only getting him the job but becoming a firm friend as well.

Winter turned to spring and by now they had saved up enough to buy a truck and a trailer. Saying goodbye to their friends they set off for America and a whole new life together.

CHAPTER FOURTEEN

Niagara Falls was their spot of choice to gain entry into the USA. Acting as if they were tourists on vacation they slipped with ease into America. When asked by us kids years later what the Falls were like they would reply, "We don't know, we were in a bit of a rush."

On entering the States my mother and father felt as though a huge weight had been lifted from their shoulders, feeling happy for the first time in a long time, thus starting a love affair with this country that would last forever more. Making their way south across one state after the other, stopping off at campsites or any place of natural beauty that caught their eye along the way, my parents would tell us of these days spent driving across this country and how they had never seen anything so wonderful in all their days: New York, Pennsylvania, Ohio, Indiana, Kentucky, Tennessee, Mississippi, to Louisiana and the Gulf, then heading west through Texas, New Mexico, Arizona, till finally reaching their destination, California.

It was here upon their arrival my mother told my father, "We are expecting our second child." My eldest brother Joseph Marshall was born in New Hall, California in 1957, New Hall being a small town in the Mohave desert just outside of Los Angeles. It was here they found themselves, after my father took some painting work from a local rancher who allowed them to live on his ranch whilst carrying out the work, after a trip to the local paint suppliers picking up a spray pump and 500 gallons of aluminum paint, with the last of their savings. This work was to serve my father as an excellent source of income for many years to follow, never looking back and never again resorting to robbery throughout the rest of his days.

After the birth of my brother this seemed to have a calming effect on my father settling down and working hard, up-grading their trailer for a far better version and trading his pickup truck for a brand new model, returning to boxing having several bouts in the professional ranks undefeated. After trading his truck for another model he went to have it registered into his name. Giving the name Tom Nelson he noticed the lady serving him had written Tom Neilson on the title deed. Telling her of her mistake the lady apologized, taking the document from my father and dropping it (in full) into the waste paper bin, before issuing him with a new one. This got my father to thinking, saying to my mother, "I wonder how many mistakes they make in a day? And just how many vehicle titles are in their rubbish bins?"

Returning that evening under the cover of darkness, he went around the back of the building, locating the large rubbish bins. Lifting the lid on one, he could not believe his eyes, for there in amongst the rubbish were hundreds of car titles with as he thought just a few lines filled out, with whoever was filling them out making a mistake and throwing it away in its entirety. Coming back later that same night but this time armed with a torch and large duffel bag he proceeded to load as many of these documents as he could carry. Getting them home and sorting them out he realized that some of them had only been filled out to the degree of the wrong date, and could easily be used again. Traveling into the next state he would rent a car using one of the newly filled-out vehicle titles as identification, then returning to California he would sell the car directly into a car sales with of course a full title of ownership.

This little enterprise was to go on very successfully for almost a year, but there was only so many rental companies in those days, so he was having to travel further and further away from Los Angeles to pick up the rentals. On one of these trips after renting the best Cadillac car the company had to offer he noticed from the clerk's reaction that something was wrong. What he did not know was that the rental company had sent out a warning to all of their dealerships to be on the lookout for anyone renting with this form of ID and if so to call the police immediately. Knowing the game was up and that the police would be there any second, he jumped in the rental car and took off for his life, just as he thought as he rounded the corner there was two car loads of police on the way to the rental firm. Thinking it will only take them a minute to realize where he was and would soon be on his tail he floored the car, knowing if he could just make it to the State line he would be home and free. Now what follows is like something out of a James Bond movie, *but I swear is true*. Heading as fast as the car would go, with police cars in chase after an obvious all-state bulletin going out across the radio, he was reaching the State line which was a river with an opening drawbridge crossing, that the police knowing if he crossed it would be out of their jurisdiction and scot free had obviously radioed ahead to have opened, therefore cutting off his means of escape. My father told the story many times of how with the lights flashing red and the bridge just opening, he gunned the car for all it was worth. Hitting the bridge at such a speed he flew across the border, landing on the other side with such a bump the wheels shot up and still spinning at such a speed warped the wheel arches of the car, forming four perfect mounds in the steel. Safely across the border he drove to the agent who bought the cars from him on a regular basis, who said "You must have had this car specially made as I have never seen those types of wheel arches before."

Reaching home he knew that it was probably time once again to gel (go) so telling my mother to pack a few things, went to sell the car and trailer to someone he knew and boarded a train to New York then caught the first boat back to England and safety.

CHAPTER FIFTEEN

On their arrival in London they purchased a new trailer and truck and not wanting to return to Scotland decided to move to the southwest of England to travel with an old friend of theirs, Willy Goodman and his family. By now my mother was expecting her fourth child, my sister Tawny who was born in Bristol hospital in 1958, just 11 months after Joseph. Working in partnership with Willy tarmacing they spent a wonderful summer traveling up and down the west country, but it was not very long till winter set in and missing the warm weather of the States and the quality of life they had left behind – with my mother telling us of not even being able to get disposable nappies for the babies in the shops at that time here in the UK, and even then the trailers in America were of a far better standard – they decided to return to the States. Taking back up where he left off with his painting work of farm barns and buildings, but this work was to one day nearly be the death of him.

While painting a stock barn roof he lost his footing, slipping on the paint and falling off of the roof some sixty foot to the ground, landing half on and half off a loading ramp with his one knee coming up and hitting him in the face, knocking him out instantly. He awoke to find himself in the hospital emergency room with, as he described, more doctors working on him then he had ever seen in his life. He had broken his back so badly that six of his vertebrae were welded together; both of his legs were also broken and the knee that had come up hitting him in the face had broken both his nose and cheekbone and fractured his skull. The doctors worked on him throughout the night, saving his life. After surgery he came to and with my mother at his bedside, having been told what happened by my father's workers, was told the news, "Sorry Johnny but your injuries were so bad we are sorry to tell you that you will never walk again."

"What?" said my father. "You must be kidding."

"No Johnny I am so sorry, but your back is so badly broken you are lucky to be alive."

After days spent in the hospital my father kept saying to my mother, “This can’t be right. If my back is so bad why can I still feel a pain in my foot?”

With his legs in traction with just the end of his toes sticking out both black and blue my mother went to get the doctor: “Sir, there must be some mistake as my husband is saying his foot is hurting him.”

“Mrs Marshall I can assure you your husband cannot feel anything, it is his mind playing tricks on him, he can see his foot is badly damaged and is thinking that must be painful.”

Taking a large needle the doctor pushed it into the end of my father’s foot, asking, “Can you feel this John?”

“No,” my father replied. They were right, he could not feel anything from the waist down.

After several weeks in hospital with the accounts department looking for payment of money they did not have, my father said, “Come back later in the early hours of the morning, bring my worker big Joe to carry me, we are getting out of here.”

“But Johnny,” my mother said, “you can’t leave, the doctors said you’re going to need more treatment.”

“Just do as I say Mary. I want out of here now.”

Big Joe was an American Indian who worked for my father and as my father has told us many times was one of the finest built men he had ever seen, He stood about six feet five and weighed over twenty stone. As the shift changed at three in the morning my mother and Big Joe came into my father’s hospital room. Picking my father up like he was a child, Big Joe carried him out to the car, laying him on the back seat and getting him home, again lifted him out, placing him in his bed. By this time my mother had sent for her sister Alice who was married to George Simmons and younger sister Rhoda who lived with them to come and help her in this hour of need. Spending just one day in bed my father said, “We have to get out of here or they will come looking for the hospital money”, so with his back in a steel brace that strapped around the whole of his body he told my mother to get him out of the bed. They carried him to the car, hooked the trailer on the back and after shaking hands with Big Joe (who lived on the park) with the words, “You take care my Indian friend”, “And you my English friend”, away they went.

CHAPTER SIXTEEN

Every day my father would have my mother pull him up onto his feet and stand him up against the wall of the trailer, leaving him for half an hour then set him back down; he would pull himself along the floor and in and out of the trailer door. Having them lift him into the pickup truck he would go calling for work, having my mother drive and ask the people if they could come outside to speak with him as he had injured his back. Within a few months he would take off his brace and again have them stand him on his feet. Half an hour went to an hour and if they were moving he would drag himself around the trailer, putting up the jacks and unplugging the electric cable. Night after night he went through this ritual, month after month, refusing to let it get the best of him; each time a bit longer on his feet, standing a bit longer without the brace, till one day a step then another… After one year my father was able to regain the use of his legs. I don't think that any other man could have done this, I think they would have resigned themselves to the fact they would never walk again, but not my father: he was determined he would walk again and walk he did. Once a fighter, always a fighter.

On his recovery my aunts and uncle returned to the UK and my father and mother carried on working and living in the States. One year later my mother gave birth to my brother, John Mark Marshall, born 1960 in Toledo, Ohio. My brother John was my hero who would die at the tender age of 25, having contacted Hodgkins disease – a form of cancer in the lymph nodes – having never smoked a cigarette in his life or drank a drink of alcohol; a powerhouse of a man, with film-star looks, who in his day was the best young fighting man amongst Gypsies. He died while I held his hand in Leeds Royal Infirmary Yorkshire, the saddest day of my life. He was a giant of a man with a heart equally big. As they say, "Only the good die young".

He left his mark on anyone who met him, with his charm, wit and sense of humor, and will always be remembered by those who loved him. I could write a book on his life and times as short as it was, but that's a story for another day.

After the birth of John my parents continued to travel throughout the whole of the United States, with them telling us in later life of the places they had visited: the Red Forest, Grand Canyon, with my father's favorite the state of Montana, known as the Big Sky Country. He would tell us of how he would sit outside his trailer at sunset and be amazed with the color of the clouds in the sky, and of how it looked as though there were a million stars. This always stood out in my memory as something I would love to see, and one day, many years later, I would.

After about a year my parents decided to take a trip back home to see their family, and also to register the birth of my brother John in the UK which was something he did with all of his children, so as we had an American birth certificate and UK one as well, and would be legal in either country. This was not as hard as you would think in those days: turning up with the child, telling the registrar they were born at home, especially in England as being a Gypsy most children were. During this time spent at home they traveled with my mother's brother Tom Buckland, his wife my aunt Evy and their family – Gracie, Mary, Tomma, Mark and Nelson – spending some time in Ireland, the men making a good living dealing in scrap metal. They said this was wonderful times as my Uncle Tom and my father were great friends throughout their lifetimes. I will always remember Tom's nickname for my father – "Saint John" – as he would laugh saying, "Look at Saint John he never does anything wrong, more like the Devil if you ask me."

Traveling back from Ireland they moved to Lewisham in London that had become a regular stopping place for my uncle and his family over the last few years, having taken a house there. This was 1963 and I remember my cousins telling me years later about going to see the Beatles at the Lewisham Odeon Theater before their worldwide fame, with my father and mother living on the local site. By now they had two more children born in the UK, my brother Lee William and sister Nicola. Also staying with them was my uncle Tommy Nelson and aunt Agnes.

During their winter stay in Lewisham the daughters of my uncle, along with most of the young Gypsy women of the area, would take a job of work at the local jam factory. During one of these work days they were to get arguing with the daughters of old Billy and May Webb who were part of a large well-renowned Gypsy family of the south of London, with both the men and women having a fearsome reputation as fighting people. One of my cousins got hit over the head with a jar as both parties traded blows, causing a huge row that escalated once back on the camping site, with the young women all shouting at each other what they were going to do and not do. The mother of the girl who hit my cousin with the glass jar came running across the site and started arguing with my uncle Tom, declaring, "I am a fighting woman and I fight men, never mind other women." Seeing this my aunt Agnes jumped to the defense of her brother and started fighting with Big May, as she was known, but being of a slight build she was no match for Big May. Thinking it was only the young girls arguing my mother was still in her trailer putting the kids to bed, but upon hearing the commotion and shouts that her sister was fighting my mother jumped from her trailer and ran to the scene of the fight. By now, seeing that his sister was fighting a losing battle my uncle Tommy had stepped in, stopping the two women from fighting. At this point, just as my mother arrived, Big May ripped off her own blouse leaving her wearing her trousers and girdle, and punching my uncle Tommy in the chest shouted, "I told you I am the best woman on this site and that I can beat a man never mind a woman." At that my mother shouted, "Well I am no man but I can beat you," and set into Big May for all she was worth. I have heard many times from everyone that was there among our family of how my mother and this woman fought – my mother was a fine built woman in her youth, standing at five feet eight, and for a woman was braver than most men – with neither woman grabbing hold or pulling hair as is the case in women fights.

They stood off from one another, trading punches like boxers, after a couple of minutes my mother getting the better of her, knocking her to the ground. "Get up," my mother said; up she got only for my mother to knock her straight back down again. "I have had enough," said Big May, with blood running from her nose and mouth. As that her husband came running with a hammer to try and hit my mother on the head. My father who had just stood back as the women fought jumped in front of his wife and with one blow knocked the onrushing hammer man spark out. After fighting Big May my mother said, "Now where is the one who caused all this?" Seeing the daughter, my mother beat her also, finishing by picking her up and throwing her in the river that ran alongside the site. Leaving the site to take the women to Uncle Tom's house, one of the

Webb women shouted, "Hey 'Yankee Johnny'," my father's nickname, "just you wait, we are sending for Black Billy."

"Send for whoever you want," was my father's reply.

CHAPTER SEVENTEEN

Not long after reaching my uncle's house while drinking a cup of tea, the door of the house came crashing in and in rushed a gang of men, with one hitting my uncle in the face with a starting handle, breaking his nose instantly. My father, seeing they were totally outnumbered, shouted, "I thought you were supposed to be proper fighting men? Who among you is Black Billy Webb?"

"I am," said one of the gang.

"Well Black Billy does it take an army of you to beat one man, or are you game enough to have a go yourself?" Thinking it would embarrass him into having a square go. The trick worked.

"I don't need any army to beat someone like you, you Yankee cunt," said Black Billy.

"Well get yourself outside then and let's see what you're made of," said my father.

Once outside both men pulled their shirts off and set to fighting. My father told us many times of how good a fighting man Black Billy was, hitting my father with good shots, with every blow he landed being cheered by his followers; but my father was no ordinary fighting man and it did not matter how many followers were there, he would never give best (declare defeat). As he would tell us boys in growing up, "Giving best is not an option, you either get knocked out or win the fight."

Seeing an opening my father stepped in with a left hook catching Black Billy clean on the jaw, and down he went. Stepping back my father said, "Have you had enough?"

"No way near," said his opponent getting back to his feet, rushing into my father but this time on unsteady legs, suffering from the effects of the knockdown. A left hook right hand and down he went again at my father's feet. This time, grabbing hold of my father's legs he shouted, "Give it to him boys!" and what was to follow would leave my father scarred for life. The gang of men who by now were heavily armed set about trying to kill my father, beating him with iron bars and pickaxe handles. If not for my mother and uncle's family jumping on top of him they would not have stopped until he was either dead or maimed for life. As that one of the gang shouted “Gavvers!” (police) and as quick as they had set into him they stopped. Getting to his feet my father run to one of his attackers who was trying to get his car started, smashing the window in on top of him with one of the pickaxe handles they had left behind, pulled him from the car in front of the police who stood back in fear of their own lives from this gang of armed thugs, and beat him unconscious. Jumping in his car he now chased his attackers down the road, attempting to run them over, with one ducking into a door way to avoid being hit, only to leave part of his arm on the wall as the car hit. My father would tell us how he drove into the doorway, trapping this man’s arm between the car and the wall, and of how the man seeing part of his hand being ripped off vomited onto the front of the bonnet. Stepping out of the car my father left him screaming and begging him to move the car to free his arm, but my father had other things on his mind: “revenge”. Reaching a telephone box my father called my uncle’s house to make sure everyone was OK, then making his way home to the site which was now deserted by the family who had attacked him, entering his trailer he tore up a towel to use as a bandage for his head and loaded his gun.

CHAPTER EIGHTEEN

Although badly injured with several large gashes on his head, my father was determined he would not go to hospital until he had dealt with the people responsible for the damage, who after the attack had run home, collected up their family and left, leaving their trailers and everything else behind. The rest of the people on the site who were not involved, and did not want to be, started hooking on their trailers (caravans) and moving, with some of them pulling up outside of my father's home to say goodbye and how they did not agree with what these people had done, asking, "What is going to happen now Johnny?"

"Well," my father said, "it's quite simple; they have until tomorrow to come back and face me or I will put a gallon of petrol and a match to everything they have left behind," knowing full well that this message would get back to his assailants.

He knew that as long as he was there these people would not return; so, telling the one man he knew was the spy in the camp he was going to the hospital and would be back in the morning, he got in his car and left. Driving up the road he turned off and stopped. As he had predicted the spy in the camp came driving by on his way to report what my father had said.

Leaving the car and now under the cover of darkness, he made his way back to the site. Slipping in unnoticed he entered his trailer and with the lights out he waited. In the early hours of the morning he could see someone crawling along the grass on his hands and knees, and then reaching his trailer standing up and making his way inside: just as he thought, this was one of the men coming back to take anything of value out of his home in case my father carried through with his threats of arson. Waiting until he was inside my father ran across, ripped open the door and jumped inside. This man looked as if he had seen a ghost, but this ghost had a loaded gun in its hand. Dropping to his knees the man started begging for forgiveness, saying, "It was not me Johnny, I had nothing to do with it. I know I was there but I never dreamed that was going to happen, please, please don't hurt me."

Without saying a word my father hit him in the face with the gun; the man tried to escape making a half-hearted attempt to get to the door but again my father brought the gun down upon his head. Grabbing him by the hair my father said, “Open your mouth.”

“What?” the man said.

“Open your fucking mouth or I will shoot you in the face.” Placing the barrel of the gun in his open mouth, my father said, “This is what I am going to do with every one of you who set about me today, one by one.”

Cocking the lever he heard a voice say, “Please don’t kill him Johnny.” Looking up, my father could see this man’s wife and children who had obviously been waiting in a car nearby and having heard the commotion came running. “Please Johnny don’t do it, don’t leave my bits of kids with no father.”

My father said he looked at this woman and her children and could see the expression of terror in their faces, looking back down to the man he noticed that he had pissed himself. It was this, he said, that brought him back to sanity, thinking: is this sniveling coward worth spending the rest of my life in prison for? “No” was the answer that came back in his head.

In one motion my father removed the gun, took a step back and kicked this man under the chin, knocking him out cold. As his wife and children ran to help him, my father walked out. Turning as he reached the door he looked back and said to the wife, “Tell him you saved his life tonight when he comes round.”

“I will Johnny I will, we don’t agree with what they did to you Johnny I promise, I am so sorry and thank you Johnny for not taking him from us.”

The next morning the site was raided by armed police who had been tipped off that my father had a gun. Thinking this might be the case my father had already hidden it under the river bank. After searching our home they allowed the people to remove their homes from the site with my father locked in the back of a police van. Many years later after hearing this man really did not take part in the attack on my father and had fallen out with his family because of it, my father would say, “Good job I didn’t mulley (kill) him.” For years the men involved in this attack went into hiding. But slowly one by one drifted back into the community, only to be confronted by my father and a good hiding

After leaving Lewisham my uncle Tom and his family made their way to Tiptree in Essex, with my cousins marrying into a family called Taylor. It was here my uncle Tom and aunt Eve was to see out the remainder of their years, leaving us with fond memories of his wicked sense of humor and love of Scotland: even after forty years in England he would say, “Can you please tell me what I’m doing living among these English pigs?” Classic.

CHAPTER NINETEEN

I was born in 1964 and named Antony Eugene Marshall: "Antony" because my father liked the name and "Eugene" after the great boxing champion Eugene (Gene) Tunney. Born with snow-white hair my father nicknamed me "Frosty".

At that time I was the youngest boy of seven children; the following year my mother gave birth to her ninth and last child, my sister Romain. Four boys and four girls: what a big family, even for those days. Still traveling back and forth from the States we settled in Bagshaw Street, Hyde, in Manchester.

One of my earliest memories is Easter egg hunting in the lane that ran alongside the house and yard; attending the local preschool, until one day walking out of the classroom and making my way home alone at the age of four, my mother having a fit when I knocked at the door and my father pinging me on the head with his stainless steel comb to boot. So back to school with my mother going mad at the teachers for allowing me to just walk out, and after she left being taken into the headmaster's office to be threatened with a small cricket bat with holes drilled through it, if I ever did it again; then, after informing my father of this, him taking me to school the next day to let the headmaster know just what would happen to him if he ever threatened one of his kids again. I mean, come on, I was only four, but this was the days of corporal punishment and such, with teachers having a full right to beat you in front of the whole class if they wanted, with pupils regularly being sent to the headmaster's office for a taste of his little holey cricket bat. After escaping again I was put in my older sister Nicky's class where I was left to draw pictures all day as the other children did their work, for her to keep an eye on me; this seemed to do the trick as I never walked out again, I guess I just needed to see a member of my family as we were all so close, with the whole eight of us kids being born within a ten-year period, with me and my brothers John and Lee being like the three amigos. We would roam freely around Hyde, picking up anything that was not bolted down and taking it home, which culminated in us hatching a master plan to steal the rabbits from the petting section of our local park, figuring out if we hid in the bushes until after the park closed we could take a rabbit each and climb up a tree that hung over the fence, dropping over the other side to our and the rabbits' freedom. But this didn't go quite as planned: by the time the gate closed it was dark and after getting the rabbits and making our ways up the tree and across the fence I slipped, with the bottom of my jeans getting caught on the fence. There I was hanging upside down with a rabbit in my arms and after a few attempts to pull me down being unsuccessful my brothers decided to go half a mile home for help – with me shouting, "One of you please stay with me it's dark and scary." But with my pleas falling on deaf ears off they went, returning a while later with my mother and father in the car, with my father lifting me off and laughing, as I still had the rabbit in my arms.

CHAPTER TWENTY

We lived a good quality of life in our little house and yard in Manchester, with my father doing well in business tarmacking and sand-blasting the front of old buildings, and us children attending the local school, it was the first time we had truly settled in one place; and with my father earning a good living we had nice tackle (cars and caravans) that in the summer months we would travel with to some of the fairs (Gypsy meeting place) across the UK.

Fairs were a great part of Gypsy tradition that sadly, slowly but surely, the councils and police closed down, with only a few of them still in operation. In my opinion this is a tragedy for the younger members of our race as they have never experienced the feeling of excitement you would have leading up to and pulling onto a fair packed with other Gypsies, meeting old and new friends alike, walking around the shows (fairground) in the day, and if you were old enough attending the local dance hall in the evening. Wonderful times. I remember one year leaving our place in Manchester and pulling on to Appleby Fair when I was about four, telling our neighbors we were off to Spain on holiday. We were pulled on the fair next to other family members and old friends of my father – Nooky Miller, Huey Burton, George Durant, and one of my father's oldest friends, Hosia Burton – and their families.

One day while watching my father and the men spinning – this is a gambling game that involves spinning two coins, preferably old penny pieces, betting on the outcome of heads or tails – all hell was to break loose, as up pulled about five truckloads of men. There was a family feud going on, as a young man had gotten married to another Gypsy man's daughter, taking as wedding gifts a new Westmorland Star trailer and Mercedes car. Now having separated from this man's daughter he decided to pull on the fair. The father took offence to this for as far as he was concerned this was his girl's home and car, not the young man's, so turning up with an army of men, instead of taking the trailer away and ladging (embarrassing) himself like he needed the money, he proceeded to smash the car and trailer to the ground. With this commotion going on everyone gathered round to watch, including my father and his friends. Now among this army of men there was one giant of a black man whose job it would seem was crowd control, walking around with a small pickaxe handle poking and pushing the people back, shouting, "Stand back unless you want some." Now my father and his friends were not people who took too lightly to being told what to do, with my father declaring, "If he pokes me with that stick I will push it up his arse."

Hearing this the black man made his way over to him and said, "What did you say?"

"You heard me," said my father; "now fuck off and pick on some cunt who will let you get away with it."

Seeing this the man who had brought the men and knowing who my father was come running over saying, "This is nothing to do with you Johnny," trying to explain the reasons for his actions, with my father saying, "I don't care what you do but tell your hired hands to go away and leave me alone."

"Who do think you're calling a hired hand?" said the black man, attempting to poke my father with his axe handle. As quick as a flash my father grabbed hold of the handle and hit this man as hard as he could on the chin, knocking him out cold, saying, "I told you to leave me alone didn't I?"

This punch would be talked about for years among people who witnessed it, as being one of the best shots they had ever seen, for this was no average man, but the best and hardest man in the area he came from. As that a full-scale battle broke out, with my father and his friends taking on these men in a pitched battle, only finishing when the riot police arrived to break it up, bringing along what I can only describe as a circus truck with cages on the back of which they were putting men involved in the fight into, my father being one of them. There was a local news television crew who had been filming the fair for the BBC that upon seeing this had turned their cameras onto the action, and after a night in the cells with no one placing charges and everyone stating they were only trying to help break up the fight, everyone was released. It was on this fair that my brother Lee was to almost lose his life also: after jumping on the back towbar of a truck to get a ride down the fair along with some friends, while attempting to jump off his jeans leg got caught on the towball. Falling backwards, he was dragged along the road on his back. If not for the actions of another Gypsy man on horseback riding alongside the truck and shouting for him to stop, Lee would have surely been dragged to his death; he was rushed to hospital but luckily only suffered cuts to his head and back and soon made a full recovery.

Returning to Manchester we were greeted by our neighbours saying, “Oh Johnny we saw you on the news fighting at the Gypsy fair, so much for being gorgers on holiday in Spain.”

Not long after this our lives were to take a drastic change, with us returning to the USA for reasons that are one of our family’s darkest secrets.

CHAPTER TWENTY-ONE

My father as I said was making a very good living from sand-blasting. This is a process of using a machine that blasts out sand cleaning the surface of old stone buildings, bringing it back to looking like new. He had started doing this work with the assistance of a local contactor and his firm after getting inquiries asking if he could do this work from a company he had done some tarmacking work for. Having hired this man's company in to sub-contract for him and seeing how it was done, my father decided he could do this work himself, and after buying the equipment set about carrying out the contracts himself. But the owner of the sand-blasting firm my father had used to start with did not like the fact that he was no longer involved and after making an approach to the customer direct to take over the work and being refused as they were more than happy with my father's service, became very angry, turning up at my father's yard one Saturday afternoon as my father and workman Bill were laying a new concrete section in the yard, declaring he wanted in, or there would be trouble, with my father telling him it was his contract to start with and his to do as he liked with, and sending him on his way, only for him to return later that day drunk into my father's yard attached to the side of our house, getting out of his truck and threatening my father.

"Go home," my father said.

"No, I warned you if you didn't let me do this work that there will be trouble and now I am telling you if you don't let me carry out this work you're going to get it."

Again my father said, "Go home, you're drunk."

Turning his back on him and walking back into the yard my father heard his workman Bill who had been with us for years shout, "Look out Johnny!"

Turning just in time he caught a glimpse of a spade as it flashed by his head, missing him by an inch. This man was now trying to attack him. Again this man swung with the spade, with my father ducking just in time.

"Stop," my father shouted. "What are you doing?"

"I am going to kill you," came the reply: again he swung the spade, this time hitting my father on the shoulder and arm. My father, by now enraged with the thought that this man was trying to kill him, flew into his attacker, managing to grab hold of the weapon and wrested it from his grip. In a mist of fear and anger he swung the spade himself, hitting his assailant on the head, killing him instantly.

Knowing that with his criminal record and medical diagnosis, if caught for this he would most likely spend the rest of his life in prison, he looked at Billy and said, "We have to get rid of the body."

"Yes," said Bill.

This man was buried under the concrete in my father's yard and his truck taken and disposed of in a scrapyard; to this day his body lies undiscovered within the yard in Bagshaw Street. My father knew that it would not be long until the police came knocking as he could not guarantee who this man had told that he was going to my father's on that fateful day, so the decision was made it was time to leave. After quickly selling up all of our positions, we made our way to Prestwich in Scotland for a plane to America. I was coming five but can remember to this day the look on my father's face as we were making our way to the airplane and were stopped by plainclothes police officers.

"Are you Mr. Marshall?" the officer in charge said.

"Yes," said my father. Knowing what I know now of what had taken place my father must have been terrified that what had happened had come to light and he was about to be arrested for murder.

The officer said, "Are these all your children?"

"Yes," my father said, thinking: where is this going?

"I am sorry to stop you but we have had a report that you are taking these children out of the country illegally and that some of them are not yours."

Someone had called up and told the police this pack of lies, obviously jealous that we were leaving to start a new life, in the hope that my father may have been arrested and not allowed to travel. This could only have come from someone close as it was only close family that we said our goodbyes to. My mother and father had their suspicions and would say about it over the years to come, but with no evidence, that's all it was: suspicions.

"Do you mind if we take a look at your passports please," said the officer.

"Of course," said my father, "there in my briefcase that you have taken from me."

The young officer holding my father's case opened it the wrong way up and all the contents fell onto the ground, including a large amount of money, as we had sold everything we owned in the world and the proceeds were in this case and strapped onto my parents in money belts. Picking up the passports the officer in charge looked at our visas; he then looked at me and said, "Who is this?" pointing to my father.

"My dad," I said, and "Who is this?" pointing to my mother: "My mam." I then continued to say, "And this is my sister Linda," and so on until I had reeled off all of the names of the whole family.

Looking at the young officer the commanding officer said, "Well what are you stood there for, pick Mr Marshall's money up and let them get on their way. Sorry for the inconvenience we have caused you today, may I commend your wonderful family, and have a lovely holiday."

And with that we boarded the plane and set off to the start of a whole new life in America.

CHAPTER TWENTY-TWO

Upon arrival in the States we made our way to the first trailer sales, buying two trailers and two trucks from the nearest Ford agents and, stopping off at a paint suppliers, purchased an airless spray painting machine and paint, then on what seemed like a big adventure to us kids, set off to find a stopping place and some work. This was 1970 and to us kids it was like going to Disneyworld. We had never seen anything like it, what with 24-hour-opening shops, trailer parks with swimming pools and pool halls, shopping malls, television with 30 channels, when in those days in England you had BBC 1 and 2 and even they closed down at 11 in the evening with the message, "We thank you for watching the BBC and wish you a very goodnight."

Coming from a three-bedroom house in Hyde to this was like a dream, when you take into account that the only excitement we had was an occasional visit to the swimming baths in Duckenfield in Manchester once a month, or a trip to the pictures in Salford was as good as it got. Moving from place to place, from state to state, spending the summers in the northern states and the winters in the southern states such as Arizona and Nevada in the west or Florida and Georgia in the east, and later on traveling north to Canada to attend the Calgary Stampede in the summer to visit my aunt Alice and uncle George who moved there not long after coming to us in the States. These were great times with us doing well and meeting new Gypsy people, and making friends who we are still in contact with to this day. One of my oldest childhood memories is playing in an orange orchard with my best friend Randle Marvin who sadly was to lose his life along with his brother Mat and several other young Gypsy men in a car crash some years later.

In the winter us kids would attend the local school wherever we found ourselves, as my father wanted us to have some education, but most of our time was spent exploring this vast and wonderful place we found ourselves in, with days spent on the beach in Florida or riding motorbikes in the deserts in Arizona, climbing up hills in Utah to find natural rock swimming holes, or wandering around the storage lots of the casinos in Las Vegas where they would keep the props for the stage shows. It was here in Las Vegas we would spend are longest stay of all during this time, living on the Purple Sage trailer park and attending Myrtle Tate elementary school. I was to find out some years later that the reason for our long stay here in Vegas was that my father had done some work for a man he had met at the Masonic lodge, who told him his brother, a fellow mason, had some work for him and would like to meet him at his home. That evening up pulled a state police car to the mobile home we were living in, and out got this man who introduced my father to his brother the sheriff.

"Mind if we talk in private?" the sheriff said to my father.

"Yes come in," said my father.

"Johnny I want to talk to you about something I hope you can help me with, and if not I know as a brother it will go no further."

"Of course," my father said.

"You see Johnny I am intending to retire soon and the owners of the casinos want to give me a little retirement fund, but I can't be seen or filmed taking this money for the reason they could blackmail me into doing something I maybe don't want to do, or turn a blind eye to, so here is my proposal: I would like to introduce you as my good friend, to carry out any work they may have, work that you can be paid highly for and you kickback my cut to me through my brother who will assist you in the works."

"I can do that," said my father, shaking his hand.

The next day my father and the sheriff went to a meeting with as my father told us, people who looked like they had just stepped off the set of *The Godfather* – eight Italian mafia men. After being introduced as his brother, the sheriff laid out his instructions to the group and left the room. "OK Johnny," said one of the Italians, "what kind of work do you do?"

"You name it I can do it, but my main works are tarmac and painting."

"OK, our managers will be in touch shortly with some requests for you to carry out some works on our behalf. Great meeting you Johnny, and thanks for your help in this matter; also any time you like you come along to the casinos and take in a show or a meal on the house."

Thanking them for the offer my father said his goodbyes and left. Within days my father was inundated with work, from the laying of asphalt on the car parks to roof repairs, lighting contracts, electrical works, even down to removal and relaying of the carpets in the hotels: so much work that my father had to bring in other companies to carry out the works, and at the end of each week the sheriff would stop by our home for his cut. He was amazed by the size of our family and would always bring with him a crate of fruit for us kids, saying, “Johnny I have never seen such good behaved children.”

He took a liking to my father I suppose because there was no questions asked and business was good. He was to go on and introduce my father to many people in the Masonic lodge as a personal friend of his, telling them if they had any work to be done and did not use my father he would take it as a personal insult, so not wanting to upset the sheriff the work would come my father’s way.

On one of the meetings in our home, after a few cans of beer, the sheriff said, “You got a gun Johnny?”

“Yeah I have a gun.”

“Got a license?”

“No I don’t have a license.”

“Well don’t worry I will get you one, but let me give you some advice: if ever, God forbid, you shoot someone for whatever reason, no matter where you shoot him, you make sure he ends up in your home and call me. We say he came into your home and tried to attack you and your wife and you shot him, and I guarantee it won’t even make court. Understand?”

I remember my father saying to my mother, “Did you hear that? He just gave me permission to get away with murder.”

This went on for some years with us doing probably the best we had ever done, with new cars, trucks and trailers and plenty of money in the bank. The sheriff even went on to get my mother a license to ducker (tell fortunes) in the state of Nevada, of which she went on to tell the fortune of Liberace the musician and several other famous people in the showbusiness world, including Nancy Austin who made all the stage outfits for Elvis Presley, who was a regular performer at the Hilton in Vegas at that time. During a visit from several of my parents’ friends from the UK and Canada my parents took them to see Elvis’s show with my mother being given one of his scarves.

At this time my older brothers Joe and John had been attending the local boxing club and after boxing successfully on quite a few occasions went on to represent the state of Nevada in the Golden Gloves nationwide tournament, with the fighter of the tournament award going to none other than Sugar Ray Leonard. It was here that I would first get to know my half-brother Johnny, my father's son from his time with Silvia, as we had left England when I was only young and only had faint memories of him. After receiving a call from my mother's sister Alice in Canada telling us that he and his wife Aggey were there and that they wanted to come to us in the states, my father traveled up to Canada and brought them back to Las Vegas, giving them one of our trailers to live in until they sorted themselves out. They had two kids: my niece Naomi and nephew Abbie. Johnny was one of the best young fighting men in England and had gotten himself into a bit of trouble back home, and as my father had done so many times, needed to get away. We were happy to see them and made them more than welcome, but Johnny was a good-looking young man who had my father's eye for the women, and after one too many late nights or sometimes not coming home at all, with too many arguments in their home that were spilling into ours, my father told him to go. Regretting what he had done the minute they left, my father searched every hotel in Las Vegas trying to find them, but to no avail: they had already caught a flight to Canada.

After a few years of their arrangement the sheriff came to see my father and said, "Johnny I am retiring next week, I want to thank you for all your help and give you some last advice. When I retire you should leave, as you know an awful lot about some people's business and I can't guarantee your safety when I leave."

"OK," said my father shaking his hand, and soon after we would leave Las Vegas, with my father never to return.

CHAPTER TWENTY-THREE

Leaving Las Vegas we again travelled around the country, with my father taking us to some of the places he had always wanted to see: again up to Canada to see our family and old friends and again making our way to the south western states for the winter, with Phoenix Arizona being the place of choice to spend the Christmas period along with all the other Gypsy families who like us were escaping the cold weather. It was here that an event would take place that would change the course of our lives.

Staying on a trailer park in a place called Apache Junction with about 50 other families, some of English dissent and some Scotch and Irish Travelers, my mother's cousin Tommy McShain had travelled down from Ontario in Canada to spend the New Year with us. Tommy was married to a non-Gypsy woman called Shirley for twenty years and they were firm friends of my mother and father. The night they arrived my parents took them out for a meal and on returning were having a drink up our trailer when in came another travelling man called Nicky Trail. The Trails are Scottish Travelers who went to the States decades ago and settled. Nicky had been drinking in the local bar with the other men on the trailer park and was a little worse for wear, but nonetheless he was a friend of my father and as such made to feel welcome. But as the night wore on he became abusive and insulting, saying to Tommy's wife, "I want to ask you something, are you a Gypsy or a Gorger (non-Gypsy)?"

"Well," the woman said, "I'm a Gorger but I have been married to this old Gypsy boy for twenty years so I like to think I am a bit of a Gypsy," trying to laugh it off.

"No you are not," replied Nicky, "you're a Gorger and once a Gorger always a Gorger."

"Hang on a minute," my father said, "you're out of line Nicky. These people are guests in my home and are not here to be insulted by you about what they are or not. Now I think it's time for you to leave."

"What, you're taking a Gorger's side over me are you?"

"No I am taking a good friend of mine's side over you. You have been asked to leave nicely once, now get out before I fucking throw you out," my father said.

As Nicky got up to leave he said, "My boys are not going to take it too kindly you throwing me out." Nicky had two sons, Nicky Jr and Sonny, who were known to be able to handle themselves in a fight, with Nicky Jr being an ex-boxing champion.

"Your boys can take it any way they like," my father said as Nicky left.

Going back to his own home Nicky started shouting, saying he had been thrown out of our home and had not said or done anything wrong and that my father had picked on him for no reasons. Me and my brothers John and Lee were playing outside with the other kids and on hearing this ran back to my father to tell him what was being said. By now Nicky Jr was in his father's trailer shouting, "Who has thrown you out? Whoever it is has me to fight," and jumping from the trailer started rounding up the rest of the men from their group trying to get a gang together.

On hearing this, my father went into the bedroom and got his handgun. Tucking it into his belt he got into his car and drove around to Nicky, who by now was jumping up and down saying what he was going to do to my father. Apart from my mother's cousin who had never had a fight in his life and my brothers Joe and John who were only young at that time, my father was on his own.

Pulling up to where these men were standing my father got out of the car and said, "What are you shouting about Nicky?"

"Did you throw my father out of your trailer?" asked Nicky.

"Yes I did," said my father, "but did he tell you why I threw him out?"

"I don't give a fuck why, you don't throw my father out of nowhere."

With one or two of the others now pitching in with a few shouts, my father said, "Whoa, hold on a minute! Which one of you wants to fight, because you can be very soon accommodated but let me tell you this, if you think for a second you're all going to set about me you're in for a big shock."

"Just what do you mean by that?" said Nicky.

As that my father pulled up his shirt revealing the 357 magnum: "This is what I mean by that," said my father. In seeing this the would-be gang shrank in size and noise, with most of them saying,

"This is nothing to do with us, we want no part of it." Even Nicky changed his tune, saying, "I don't even know what this is all about Johnny. Can you please tell me what we are arguing about? We have always gotten along in the past."

"Oh I will tell you what this is about, your father is a cheeky old cunt, coming into my home and insulting my wife's family."

"Well," said Nicky, "if that's the case he deserved to be thrown out and can we shake hands and forget about it."

"Fair enough," said my father.

We went on to have good Christmas and new year and then went our separate ways. But this would not be forgotten by the Trails, and would be brought up sometime later, once again culminating with my father being charged with attempted murder.

CHAPTER TWENTY-FOUR

Moving to Salt Lake City, Utah, stopping at a trailer park next door to the state fairground, and on the banks of the Jordan River. Utah is the home of the Mormon religion. My father was to do very well here in business as not a lot of Travelers had been here before, thinking it was very strict because of the religious side of things, but this did not affect my father. If anything, he played on the fact that people took him for a Mormon, what with the large family of kids and such. Us younger kids would spend wonderful days here swimming in the river that run along the back of the trailer park, or choring (stealing) into the fairground; even when closed this was a great place to play and explore. I can remember choring in through a hole in the fence to see the top Country and Western stars of the day perform there: Tammy Wynette, Lynn Anderson, Tanya Tucker, and Ray Stevens, who had a big hit song at the time called 'Misty', with Lynn Anderson singing 'Rose Garden'.

Everything was going well until one day the Trail family pulled onto the park. Now as far as we were concerned this argument was finished and it seemed that way to start, with Old Nicky and young Nicky coming over and shaking hands with my father. Life went on as normal, with the men all going out getting a good living and the women and children getting along fine, but what we had not taken into account was Nicky's younger son Sonny, who had not been present at the Christmas time, and had apparently taken the throwing out of his father as a personal insult to him and he wanted to do something about it. One evening after returning from work my father was sitting up his trailer having just had a shower, while my mother made his dinner. I can remember this like yesterday as he used to get a bit sunburned and I would push my hand against his belly, seeing it left a white mark where my hand was when taken away, and we would laugh together over this, with him saying, "Do it again Frosty," only to say, "Look at this Mary" and laugh again, sending me down to the store at the front of the trailer park to get some cold drinks for us.

As I got there I happened to notice some of the traveling men from the camp coming out of the bar next door, with one of them saying, "I will show you what I am going to do with him tonight," and then proceed to shadow box, throwing punches at his imaginary opponent.

Leaving the shop and heading back to the trailer, I passed these men that were now walking down the camp towards our trailer, and the one who was shadow boxing was none other than Sonny Trail. On seeing this I ran as fast as I could. Getting home I began telling my father what I had seen, with my father just nodding. As that a knock came to the door.

"Come in," my father said, and in walked Sonny Trail and two of his cousins: Eddy Boswell, who had stopped with us on many occasions, and one other.

"Hello Johnny," they said, "we have come to ask you to go for a drink with us."

My father, armed with the information I had given him, said, "Not tonight fellas, I have only just got back from work and haven't even had my dinner yet, but sit down and have a chat for a minute and Mary will make you a cup of tea." With my father looking at me, "Why don't you go play pool with the boys?" he said, knowing what he was telling me without saying it.

I left the trailer and run to the pool hall at the front of the camp where my older brothers were playing pool with two girls. Telling them as quick as I could of what I had seen and what was happening we dashed outside and into my brother Joe's pick-up truck. Heading back to the trailer we passed these men walking back to the bar; pulling up outside our trailer we walked in to find my father pulling on his boots. "What happened?" my brothers asked, and my father told us that Sonny had said, "You threw my father out of your trailer last Christmas Johnny, do you think you could throw me out?"

My father replied, "There isn't a man walking I couldn't throw out of here Sonny."

At that my mother said, "Now hang on a minute you lot, my kids are in this trailer and the best thing you can do is get the fuck out."

"We haven't come here to fight in your trailer Mary," said Eddy.

"Well," my father said, "if it's a fight you want a fight is what you will get, get yourselves here first thing in the morning and we will have it. Now fuck off out of my home."

As that they got up and left. Now my father was many things but patient was not one of them, and thinking by tomorrow they would have a few more of their family there and we would be hugely outnumbered, he walked into the bed room and loaded his handgun. With the boys throwing a couple of baseball bats into the boot (trunk) my father, mother and two brothers drove up to the bar. Entering the bar my father said, "Never mind tomorrow morning, get yourself outside fighting man" to Sonny, who looked a bit shocked at this turn of events that the odds were now in my father's favour.

"Hold on Johnny I thought we were fighting in the morning."

"We are fighting now," said my father as he back-handed him across the mouth, "get outside."

Now this was 1975 and my father was in his late fifties but still as game as ever, with Sonny being only 22 and trained to death knowing this fight was coming up, standing at over six feet and at least two stone heavier than my father. "Let me fight him," my brother Joe said, who at this time was 17 years old, and a very skilled fighter.

"No it's my fight, you're too young and he is too heavy for you," my father said. "I will have him."

CHAPTER TWENTY-FIVE

Now out in the car park Sonny and my father set to fighting, with the other men standing back watching. Trading shot for shot my father was doing good, landing a right hand and staggering Sonny. Again a left hook, right hand and Sonny went down. Rising to his feet my father stepped in to finish him off only to get caught with a hammer of a blow, knocking him down. Getting up my father fought on, but as is the case with so many older men their pride keeps them going, and as the old saying goes, "Old man time waits for no one." It was instinct alone that was keeping him on his feet.

Seeing this my brother John, who at 14 was the most dangerous of young men you would ever come across, opened the boot and removed the baseball bats, passing one to Joe. He stepped forward and hit Sonny straight in the forehead, knocking him out instantly. Not content with this, for in their eyes beating their father, John and Joe proceeded to beat him with the bats until he lay motionless on the floor. Sonny's cousin run forward attempting to stop them only to be beaten also, with John running at the other cousin who turned on his heels and run. As this Sonny's father and brother came running across the car park shouting, with young Nicky holding a weapon in his hands. Seeing this my mother jumped from the car with the handgun, shooting it into the air then pointing it at them, "Stop right there or I will blow your fucking heads off. Get in the car," she said to my father and brothers, then with the sound of sirens in the back ground sped off, knowing the police would be on them within minutes.

My father drove across the Jordan River Bridge adjacent to the camp and threw the gun and bats into the water, turned around and drove straight home. Within seconds up pulled the gavvers (police) who arrested all of them. Holding them overnight they released my mother and brothers, but charged my father once again with attempted murder. "With Sonny in such a bad way," the police told him, "it's touch and go, and if he dies you will be charged with murder."

The next day we got a call from Eddy asking to see my mother, who told her and Joe that he and the others would not be making any statements, and just wanted it to be over with, so with Sonny pulling through, and no gun to be found or weapons of any kind in the car, after posting a bail bond my father was bailed. Three weeks later an ambulance brought Sonny back to the trailer park. I remember seeing him and thinking he looked like the "invisible man" covered in bandages from head to toe. After getting permission to move to another camp from the police as my father was on bail, we left the camp. Sonny Trail was never to recover from his injuries and, so I believe, to this day struggles to live a normal life.

After leaving the camp still bailed to return some weeks later, my father once again decided to put some distance between him and the police, so selling everything apart from our Mercury Colony Park station wagon, we headed to New York and using our Nelson passports booked passage for my mother and sisters along with the car on the QE2, splitting us up for safety with him and us boys hopping on a plane to London Heathrow.

It was now 1976 and I still recall coming off the plane at Heathrow and having to travel through the centre of London en route to Tiptree in Essex, the hometown of my mother's brother Tom Buckland and his family. I remember thinking how different it all seemed, with the cars being so small, the old double-decker buses, and black cabs. Passing Marble Arch, Piccadilly Circus, stopping off at a fruit stall to pick up some gooseberries that we had never seen before, then heading out the A12 towards Colchester, finally reaching Tiptree that afternoon, with my father and two older brothers staying with my Uncle Tom and Aunt Eve, with me and my brother Lee stopping at Tom's girls, my cousin Mary who is married to Jimmy Taylor, and Tomma who is married to Nelson Taylor, who both had children of similar ages to myself: Jimmy, Harry, Sherry, Michelle, Levi and Markey. While their children were in school me and Lee would go along with Mary and Tomma who would take great pride in introducing us to the local village people as their cousins from America.

I think back on these as happy times and on the many occasions I have traveled back to Tiptree I still smile at these memories. 1976 was one of the hottest summers on record for the UK and the time I spent there with my cousins will stay with me forever. Renting a house in Queen Street in preparation for my mother and sisters arriving, my father set to getting ready to go back to work, but before this it was decided we would rent two small trailers and along with my Uncle Tom, Aunt Eve and Mary and Jimmy we would travel around the UK attending fairs to see old friends and family, moving first to Scotland and Musselburgh races in Edinburgh, pulling onto the middle of the racecourse. Gypsy fairs always coincide with major race meetings or summer festivals and have been a tradition for centuries for British Gypsies: fairs like Epsom for the Derby, York for the Trebor meeting, Doncaster for the St Ledger. In years gone by fairs would dictate your moving habits, taking you from one end of the UK to the other. They started as meeting places for the men to trade in horses and for the families to get to know one another; also, as is the case in most Gypsy weddings, a great place to meet your future husband or wife. These were wonderful events that sadly have all but died out due to the councils and police closing them down. I remember as a young man along with my brothers and sisters the excitement we would feel in anticipation of pulling onto one of these fairs, and of the feeling of sadness when it was finished and we were pulling off saying goodbye to friends we had met, only to feel the same way as the next fair approached.

In the summer of 1976 England was experiencing a heat wave the likes as had never been seen before, and I recall after hearing all the stories from my parents of how cold and miserable it was, thinking it's not so bad; but summer is summer and the winters were a whole different story. Pulling first onto Musselburgh Fair in Scotland my father set to buying us a new big trailer from one of the dealers who would be in attendance at these occasions, deciding on one called a Portmaster and buying it from Dick Cunningham from Doncaster, whose wife was a relative of my mother, being from the Penfold family.

I remember walking into this trailer for the first time with my mother to have a look around. Now bear in mind we had just returned from the States, where we had a 37-foot Travel Ease American trailer with two tip outs (slide-out rooms) front and back, large fridge freezers, plumbed-in baths and showers, and central heating. And now we were standing in what I could only describe as a box on wheels filled with mirrors, asking my mother, "Is this it? Where's the fridge freezer?", with her pointing to a cupboard with a fridge the size of a matchbox in it, and "What is this?" I said, looking at the fireplace.

"That's the coal fire, it will be your job to light it and keep it going when we need it."

I remember thinking to myself you have got to be kidding and even at that age realizing how far behind this country was from the US at that time, but the trailer was bought and needless to say I became an expert fire tender.

Moving on we pulled to Doncaster Races, then from there to old Joe Cunningham's camp in Tilts Lane. This camp even to this day remains a regular stopping place for my family after all these years. That year we made the rounds of all the fairs and after seeing old friends and family members we settled down to the business of earning our living, with my father deciding we would do sludging (roofing) work – this was a form of roof coating with a rubberoid material – also tarmacking and barn painting. But after being out of the country for so many years my father struggled to fit back into the run of things, and it was always in the back of his mind that he really did not want to be here and if not for the problems in America we would still have been there.

After pulling from the north of England we made our way to Orpington in Kent where my father rented a large house from a local doctor and finally started getting into the run of things. Work was good and he had bought a new Bedford TK Truck and Ifor Williams cattle box to carry our tarmac equipment, when one evening we would get a call from someone giving us the bad news about my half-brother Johnny. Johnny and Aggie had returned from Canada and were stopping at Berwick-upon-Tweed on the camp of a man called Hustle Drummond. The tale goes that Johnny was messing around with this man's daughter and after being approached by this man to stay away from his girl, with the answer being, "Go fuck yourself, I do what I want," this man's two sons attempted to attack Johnny, but were no match for him as Johnny was a fighting man of a very high caliber, and quickly disposed of their threat, beating the two of them in one go, knocking them both out in the pub, only for them to return that evening with their father, knocking at Johnny's door saying, "Come out, you have got to fight again." Johnny knowing these men were no good to him jumped out of his trailer door and said, "OK which one of you wants it first?" Looking to the older brother who was standing to his left he could see by the look on his face that something was not right and as that he looked back to the father who by now had got out of the car and was holding a shotgun aimed at him, with Johnny jumping out of the way but not quick enough to miss the blast of the gun as it hurled in his direction, catching him in the legs and knocking him off his feet. But as luck would have it the gun was of an older type and only a single shot.

With the words, "You're dead now, I am killing you tonight," Hustle re-loaded. Not able to get to his feet because of the serious injuries to his legs Johnny crawled under his trailer, by now everyone on the camp was out wondering what was going on, and with old Hustle trying to get another shot at him he was tackled by other men on the camp and disarmed. Johnny was rushed to Newcastle Hospital by now at risk of losing his life due to the large amount of blood loss, for the shell had ripped into his thigh and severed a main artery. On hearing the news my father and mother jumped on a plane and made their way to Newcastle as quick as they could. Arriving there my father spoke with the main doctor and asked what they intended to do. "Well Mr Marshall we have got the blood loss under control and are now fighting to save his leg."

After some hours the doctor came to speak with them again, telling my father that they had exhausted every avenue at their disposal and in their opinion the leg would have to be removed, and that the only doctor who might be able to save the leg was a specialist in London. My father said, "I will pay whatever costs are involved, please try and save my boy's leg."

After another meeting with the doctors it was decided that Johnny would probably not make the flight, due to more complications that had arisen. Going into Johnny my father told him all that the doctors had said and the choice was his to make if he wanted to try and get to London my father would fly with him, but if something went wrong in the air he would lose his life. Throwing the blankets back and looking at his leg that by now was as black as coal due to all the blood loss, Johnny looked at the doctor and said, "Take it off."

I remember my father telling us of how Johnny was taken down to surgery sitting up and came out sitting up saying, "It's gone dad they cut my leg off. But I would rather go through life with one leg than be dead." Hustle Drummond handed himself into the police and even though he admitted to the crime, with Johnny not attending court or giving evidence he received a small sentence, and upon his release went into hiding and was never seen again.

CHAPTER TWENTY-SIX

The following year we attended Musselburgh fair again, pulling on with our new trailers, truck and Datsun pickups that were all the rage of this time, and Johnny pulling on alongside of us with his wife and kids.

Going to the pub one night with an old friend of his, Jacky Low, Johnny was confronted by two members of a notorious traveler family, these men were noted Scottish fighting men of this time, ferocious warriors who rule Scotland to this day.

"Hey Johnny," one said, "Is it right you got your leg shot off?"

"Yea, that's right," Johnny said.

"Well I guess that's put an end to your fighting days, eh."

"Yea," said Johnny, "it looks that way," biting his lip, as in his prime neither one of these men would have been a match for him.

"Well, wee man, the best thing you can do is get out of this pub before we rip that false leg of yours off and stick it up your arse."

With no other option but to get up and leave, Johnny came to my father telling him what had taken place, saying "None of them would dare open their mouths to me when I had both my legs, now I have to suffer the indignity of this."

"Not as long as I am alive," was my father's reply, so along with the Lows they drove down the fair in search of these people. Coming upon their trailers my father shouted "Where are these fighting men who like to try and take liberties with people, come on out and see if you can take the same liberties with me."

Half expecting there to be some retaliation for their insults to Johnny in the pub these men had gathered all their men together and on hearing my father shouting came running out ripping their shirts off.

"Who wants to fight!" they shouted. "We can beat anyone of you."

As one of them approached the crowd my brother Joe flew into him, hitting him with shots from every angle, knocking him down only for him to scramble to his feet and run at Joe. Knowing that Joe was far too fit for him to box with, he had to take it to the ground using his superior weight advantage and strength. But no sooner did they hit the floor, my father pulled them up: "Fight fucking fair," he demanded.

By now a full scale battle was underway with members of both sides pairing up and getting to it, and our team was winning. Seeing this, the leader of these men ran back towards his trailer and what happened next is talked about in gypsy fighting folklore to this day. Thinking that their leader and elder statesman had fled, most of the other combatants decided to follow suit, then after hearing what sounded like a motorcycle being started, out stepped the leader with a large chainsaw in his hands.

"Now you're all going to die!" he shouted walking towards my father and other members.

Reaching inside the back of our pickup my father pulled out a shotgun, aimed it at him and pulled the trigger, spraying him with lead shot. He dropped the chainsaw and ran for cover, now all rules were forgotten, and what was to follow would end up in a blood bath, with members of both sides being taken to hospital with serious injuries. But by now there was a large police presence, with a commanding officer telling all who would listen that he would arrest anyone involved in any further fighting immediately.

Travelling on From Musselburgh we returned to our home in London and after a visit from my cousin Joe Kennedy and his family who had lived in Australia for many years, my father decided we would take a trip down under to see it for ourselves.

My half-brother Johnny, sadly, many years later lost the battle with his demons within; he was found dead of a drugs overdose in his home in Manchester.

CHAPTER TWENTY-SEVEN

Selling our trailers and vehicles, we boarded a Qantas airlines flight to Sydney, Australia, and were greeted by Joe Kennedy, his wife Eunice and four children: Blanch, Josephine, Sally and John, named after my father. After the two years spent in England this was like a breath of fresh air for our family. Quickly buying new trailers and trucks we took up residency in a place called Narrabeen on the coast just outside of Sydney, a beautiful place, a stone's throw away from the beach. This felt more like home to us after so long spent in the States, and we soon settled into the rhythm of things, doing painting of house roofs. Work was easy and life was good.

Traveling north along the Gold Coast we made our way to Brisbane, stopping off along the way at Coffs Harbour, Tweed Heads, and Surfers Paradise. To me it seemed like paradise. Coming fourteen I was going out to work in the morning and then spending the rest of my days on the beach with my brothers and sisters, then out in the evenings to the milk bars and many restaurants that were to be found along the shoreline. It was on one of our visits to the beach that I had my one and only encounter with sharks. Swimming out to a reef with four of my siblings about one hundred meters from land, we were snorkeling around the reef that you could stand on, when out of the corner of my eye I caught a glimpse of a large fin. Standing on top of the reef I removed my mask to have a better look when to my shock and horror out of the water popped the fin again, closely followed by another. For a split-second I thought it was my mind playing tricks on me, but it did not take longer than that to realize I was not seeing things and we were in trouble.

Shouting to the rest of the kids "SHARKS!!" I started swimming back to shore. On reaching the beach I saw to my amazement that the others had thought I was joking and had not moved an inch, shouting again, "Get out of the water there are two sharks in there," only to hear my brother Lee say "Well I can't hear the theme from *Jaws*," and start to sing "Der Dum Der Dum Der Dum", typical Lee sense of humor. Now losing my temper I shouted, "Get out of the fucking water: I am telling you I have seen sharks."

Finally realizing I was not joking they all made it safely back to shore. A memory that will stay with me forever is looking along the beach and as far as you could see, people running out of the water in waves as word reached them of there being sharks in the water. Making our way up onto the pier next to where we were swimming we watched as the sharks swam up and down the beach line. On hearing there was a problem on the beach my father and mother came running to make sure we were OK, joining us on the pier. I was in mid-argument with a surfer who was trying to convince everyone that they were not actually sharks but dolphins. "Well," my father said, "if they're dolphins you won't mind me throwing you off the pier in alongside them will you?" only for the man to say, "No mate I am not that sure," as he made his retreat.

That Christmas we made our way to a place called Wagga Wagga in New South Wales, as this was the place that all the Gypsies in Australia had decided upon to get together to spend the Christmas and New Year. Pulling onto the trailer park we were greeted by dozens of other Gypsy families many of whom we already knew, and many that on hearing we were in Australia had come along to meet us. Even some old friends from the States that were now in Australia had made their way to come and spend some time with us. With the older people attending the working men's club, us youngsters made are way to the local disco. This was 1978 and fully in the disco era, the days of *Saturday Night Fever*, with bands like the Bee Gees, Chic, Village People, and Donna Summers all having hits in the charts, with every young Gypsy man thinking he was John Travolta, flared trousers and wide-necked collars to boot. We had a wonderful time meeting some new friends who would remain to this day, and after celebrating the New Year of 1979 returned to Sydney and the camp at Narrabeen. Not long after this my father's brother Dids and his family also came to Australia making it their home, to this day they can be found just outside of Sydney, with my uncle only returning in his last days, coming back to the place of his birth on the Galloway borders of Scotland. My aunt Dinah's brother Cec Waters also immigrated to Australia with his three sons, Guy, Troy, and Dean, who went on to be Commonwealth boxing champions, all fighting for world titles, only to lose on split decision, with Troy fighting the likes of Gianfranco Rossi, Terry Norris, and Simon Brown. He was inducted into the Australian Boxing Hall of Fame in 2009.

Within a year we would return to the UK as my elder sisters were in their late teens and early twenties and wanted to come back home as most Gypsy girls do to find an English Gypsy husband, so once again we found ourselves in England, this time renting a house in Leeds, Yorkshire, until such time as we acquired new trailers and cars. After buying two new Land Rovers, one van and one station wagon and two big trailers – one being a Marshall and the other an Arrow – with us boys having a smaller tourer as our bedroom, we again set off on our travels, ending up on Hoolie Burton's site at Selby, in between York and Doncaster in South Yorkshire.

By now I was fifteen and had just started driving, with my first car being a Land Rover pick-up with a six cylinder engine and a Fairey Overdrive. I could hardly afford the petrol to run it as it was a gas guzzler, but I loved it all the same, washing and polishing it on an almost daily basis. I had bought it from my brother John who had taken ill at this time and was under a specialist in Leeds having tests done.

September came and with it Doncaster races, which we never missed, going to work and not returning till late. I traveled the short distance from Selby to Doncaster on my own that evening to attend the dance, knowing that my brothers and sisters would meet me there, turning up outside the night club that was known as the "sweat box", for the reason that the owners would cram as many people in as they possibly could until the condensation would drip from the ceiling, landing on the crowd's head below. Whilst queuing up, a group of much older traveling boys attempted to jump the queue, and after being turned away by the doormen for being well known to them as trouble causers, decided to vent their anger at the on-watching crowd, with me being singled out for special attention. I suppose the fact I was wearing bright red jeans and T-shirt with red and white training shoes did not help my cause, but with us having traveled the world, we were known for our stylish and modern sense of dress. But this was Doncaster in Yorkshire and the sweat box, not the bright lights of London.

"Oh," said one of these men, "look at this one with his fancy clothes. I bet you think you're a fighting man," said this man who at this time would be in his early twenties. Along with him was his brother and three other men from another well-known family in Yorkshire. Coming closer then stopping, he again said, "Because see fighting men like you I would knock out with one punch."

Now I am fifteen years old and on my own, faced with five men that I knew if I started fighting with one of them, they would all pitch in and kick me to death, so the only option open to me was run or fight and running is not in my breeding. So looking at a friend of mine who had just left my brothers in the bar of the Danum Hotel, I said, "Go get the boys," and off he ran. Knowing help was on its way my thoughts were to hit this man and do my best to stay on my feet until the cavalry arrived. Just as this up pulled the police who had been called by the night club bouncers, who could see what was happening through the door windows. With this the would-be attackers slipped around the corner and ran into the night.

Just then my brothers John and Lee came running down the road. "What's going on?" John said. As I was telling them the story who came back around the corner trying to blend in with the crowd? None other than the one who wanted to fight me. Seeing this I walked over and said, "Hey you, I do think I am a fighting man, what do you have to say now that your little gang is not here anymore?"

"I don't know what you are talking about mate," came his reply.

"Let me tell you what he is talking about mate," said my brother John, "you thought, you and your mates were going to set about a fifteen-year-old boy, well this fifteen-year-old boy has brothers, who are fighting men," and as that hit this man with probably the hardest punch I have ever seen, lifting him off of his feet and knocking him straight through a shop plate glass window, out cold. Seeing this the doormen opened the doors and said, "Come in boys before the police come and lock you up." Looking at my brother John the bouncers said, "What a shot fella and didn't he deserve it." Looking at me one of them said, "I will tell you what, this young one's game, he wouldn't run, but don't worry if they would have started on you we would have come out and helped."

After about an hour in the club the doormen came to where we were sitting, saying, "Listen boys I think you better know there are about a hundred men outside trying to get in to you, they won't get through the door, but you know they're gonna be waiting on you when you go outside."

My brother John looked up and said, "One hundred of them eh, have you got a back door?" Making us all laugh.

"As it so happens we do," said the doorman, leading us through the loft space over the top of the adjacent stores, and down a fire escape at the back of the building. "You take care boys," said the doorman as we walked away.

Some years later I was to meet up with these men again when they pulled onto a camp along with an old family friend of ours, Aunt Winnie Kelly and her children. I was staying on this camp by myself, I was seventeen by now, but give them their dues they never mentioned the fight again, and we went on to spend a nice summer together. Shortly after the fight at Doncaster, my brother John was taken ill, and after finding a lump in his upper chest area, was diagnosed with having Hodgkin's disease, a rare form of cancer, and was attending Leeds Royal Infirmary, having to undergo courses of chemo and radiation therapy.

CHAPTER TWENTY-EIGHT

During our stay at Selby a lifelong friend of ours called Billy Dale, who we had first met in Canada, came to visit us, telling us of a new job he was doing that he had picked up in the USA, dealing in waste oil. Basically it involved the finding of waste oil that was in abundance in the UK in those days. With most companies paying a fee to have it collected from their facility, they were more than happy to give it to you for free. This product we would sell back to the oil refineries for in the region of 38 to 40 pence per gallon.

Starting off with 1,000-gallon tanks built into the back of transit vans we set off in search of this black liquid gold. It was no problem to go out in a day and fill and empty these tanks three to four times a day, bringing in a profit of about £1,300 a day after expenses, £7,800 per week. This was the early eighties and to be bringing in that kind of money per week for the average Gypsy man was unheard of, let alone a 17-year-old boy. As I got older, me and my brother John became increasingly close, working as partners in our new oil venture. With him being too ill at times to even get out of bed, I took the responsibility of being the bread winner for both of us, and was more than happy to do so, making sure that every penny I earned he had his equal share. Business was good and there was more than enough for both of us. Apart from his illness these were good times, as after a period of time we had our set suppliers from whom we would get our supply of waste oil, loading in the early hours of the morning and most of the time being finished by 10 am, allowing us the rest of the day to spend at our leisure: going to concerts, the cinema or shopping which was one of our favorite pastimes, being young men with a taste for expensive clothing, jewelry, and fast cars.

At this time we were living in Scotland on the camp of Andrew Young, whose father was an old friend of ours that he had met during his time in borstal. It was here I would meet one of my oldest friends, Bobby Rowan from Falkirk in Scotland. From the minute we met we got on like a house on fire. He was a top amateur boxer representing Scotland at the highest level, and one of the only people I would class as a true friend. I have not seen him in many years, but look forward to the day we meet again. As young men, we would spend our weekends in Newcastle-upon-Tyne, as my brother John was going out with a girl who he would end up marrying called Pamela Hopkinson, whose brother Adam was a good friend of mine. Newcastle was a hive of activity at this time, with its clubs and bars being the best in the UK, namely Tuxedo Junction, that had won awards for being the best night club in Europe. These were great times spent with good friends of mine, Adam Hopkinson and Joe Reilly.

By now two of my elder sisters and one brother had gotten married, with my sister Linda marrying Jimmy Mulroy from South Shields, Joe marrying Deborah Rains from Newcastle, and my sister Tawny marrying our second cousin Bobby Kennedy, with John soon to follow marrying Pamela. Turning eighteen and thinking I was going to live the playboy lifestyle for many years to come, I was to meet someone who would change my way of thinking.

In the summer of 1983 we children who were still at home would once again attend Cambridge Fair in June, booking into a hotel for the main four days. We met up with some boys named Bobby and Tommy Frankham, who would become good friends of me and my brother Lee. One day while walking around the fair with Bobby, up pulled a car with a boy that was known to me, with what I can only describe as the most beautiful girl I had ever seen sitting next to him. Asking Bobby if he knew who she was, he said, "She's my cousin Lila Doe."

"Well introduce me to your cousin Lila Doe," was my reply. Now I had heard of the saying "love at first sight", but quite frankly, thought it was a load of bullshit, but on walking up to the car, me and this girl's eyes met, and the electricity between us could have powered London.

After saying hello, she then asked me, "What's your name?"

"I am Tony Marshall."

"Oh you're Tony Marshall," she said in a strange way. Little did I know, but the boy she was going out with must have known we would like each other, and had told her she was not allowed to speak to me. Well you know what they say about forbidden fruit. Oblivious to everyone else's conversation we talked until her boyfriend had finally had enough and drove away.

That evening seeing her in the night club, she was a vision of everything I wanted in a woman, with long brown hair down to her waist, chocolate colored skin, and the most beautiful brown eyes. I thought, "Boyfriend or not she's going to be mine." Walking over I grabbed her by the hand, "Come on let's dance," leaving him stood there watching. I said, "I think you are beautiful."

"Thank you," she replied.

"Too good to be going out with him," I said, pointing to where he was standing. "Finish with him and go out with me," I asked. Within twelve months we were married.

After turning up to see her one weekend, I said, "I got you a present," handing her a large gift wrapped box. Opening it to reveal a boy cabbage patch doll with a little cloth bag tied to its wrist, "What's in the bag?" she said.

"Open it and see," I replied. Inside was an engagement ring. I had picked out with the help of my sister Tawny and brother in law Bobby that week. Stepping out of the car I got down on one knee and asked her to marry me, "Yes," she said and the rest is history.

Now as anyone who has ever had a cabbage patch doll will tell you, they come with a birth certificate that you fill in with the name of your choice. Taking a pen Lila wrote "Antony Santino Marshall", the name we had agreed to call our first child, as we were both in agreement that we would only have sons and lots of them. People who know me will be laughing by now.

After spending our honeymoon in London, we travelled back to the camp I was stopping on with my family, near Manchester. Speeding north in my Ford Escort XR3 that was the young man's car of the day, up alongside us pulled an unmarked police car, signalling me to pull over. Stopping on the hard shoulder with the police car in front out got a chief inspector with his braided cap on. Walking towards us a truck came by and blew his hat into the middle of the road; I swear cars and trucks were swerving to run it over. After some time the officer retrieved his hat that was now squashed to pieces, and with a face like thunder walked up to my window: "Do you know what speed you were doing?" he said.

"No I'm sorry, Sir."

Cutting me short he said, "And you young lady, you are sitting so close to him I thought there was only one person in the car."

"Officer," Lila said, "I am so sorry it is my entire fault. We have just got married, and I am so excited. We are traveling to meet his family and we cannot stop smiling, talking and laughing. So you see officer it is my fault for distracting him from his driving."

"Well," said the officer, "congratulations to you but put your seat belts on and slow down or you won't be seeing anyone, never mind his family. Now get on your way and have a nice life." The powers of a woman!

After a few weeks in Manchester we moved on to Skipton in Yorkshire and then back to Newcastle. Returning from work one day I walked in to see Lila sitting smiling.

"I have some news for you," she said, "we are going to have a baby."

This was like music to my ears, as I had found the love of my life and children would be the cherry on the cake. Walking into my brother John's trailer I said, "Guess what, you are going to be an uncle."

Jumping from his seat he grabbed and cuddled me and Lila, saying, "Oh I am so happy for you both, that's the best news I have had in a long time."

"Well get ready for some more," I said, "we want you to be its godfather."

I will never forget the look on his face, a look of pride and love that will stay within my heart for ever more.

Signpost in the Netherlands telling gypsies will be flogged and branded

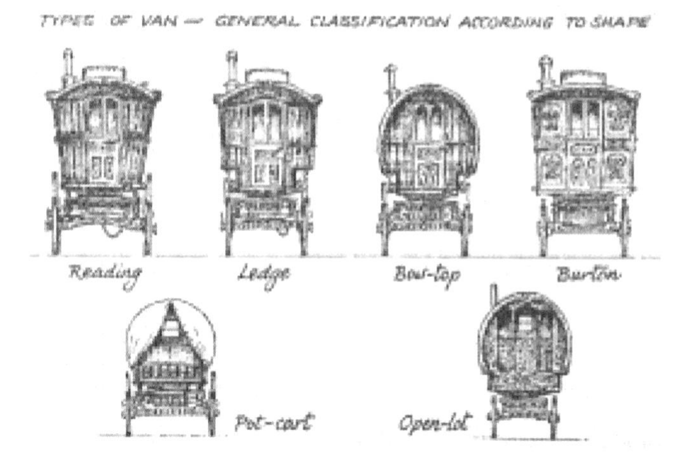

Types of gypsy wagons

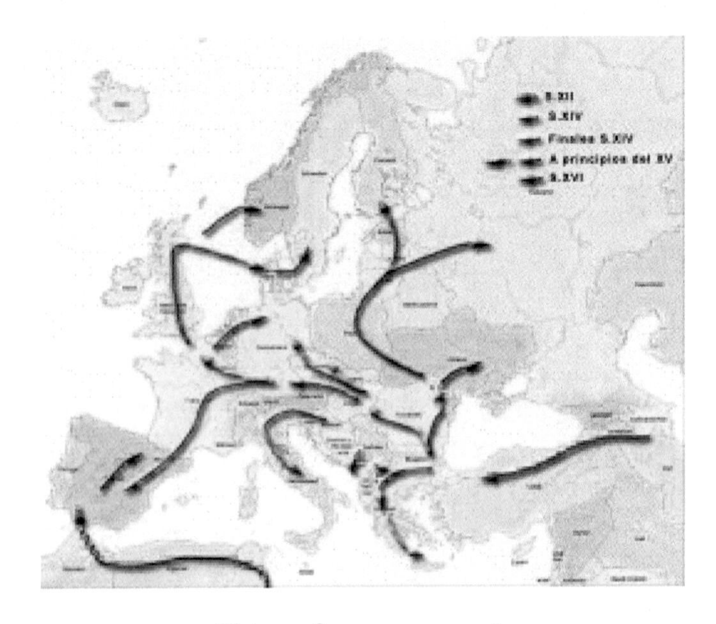

History of gypsy movements

Camp Painting by Charles Bonnet

Reading Wagon

Van Gogh painting

Dad in his boxing days

My brother John

Dad, Mam and us kids

Me and Lila

Me in Dubai

Me, Lila Tawny and Montana

Amber and Narny's wedding day

Lila Tawny and James wedding day

Montana and Joe's wedding day

Jade and Billy's wedding day

King Billy's Cemetery

King Billy's Grave

CHAPTER TWENTY-NINE

Moving on from Newcastle we found ourselves once again returning to Doncaster for the winter, pulling onto an old friend of ours' camp called Wickwack Burton, in Stockbridge Lane, Bentley, Doncaster. Sitting in John's trailer one night he said, "Let's go on holiday together, somewhere warm."

"OK," I said, and the following day Lila and John's wife Pamela booked us to go to Ibiza for a week. This was long before it turned into the rave party capital of the world, and was still a nice place to go for a quite break away. This was one of the best weeks of our lives, spending the days on the beach or around the pool, then in the evenings we would get dressed up and head out to the restaurants or shops. One of my fondest memories is upon our return while driving back home from the airport my brother John singing along to the George Michael song "Careless Whisper". Lila by now being five months' expecting, Christmas time came and went and while making plans for where to go for the New Year's Eve, I was to make one of the biggest mistakes of my life.

Sitting with John he said, "Where are you going for New Year's? Why don't you go with the rest of the kids to the party in Birmingham?"

"Oh I don't know," I said.

"Don't be silly you're still only young, go and have a nice time instead of sitting with us old fogies," he said, and so we went, but little was I to know it was to be my brother John's last, and I so wish I had spent that precious time with him.

After the New Year me and Lila moved to Chester to be near my sister Tawny and brother-in-law Bob and his family, as his father Johnny had not long passed away, dying of a massive heart attack whilst driving to work one day. It was here that Lila would have our first child. Coming home from work one day I was greeted by my aunt Bella, Johnny's wife, telling me that Lila had been rushed to hospital, and the baby was on its way. This was well before mobile phones, so she had no way of letting me know. Reaching the hospital and finding what ward she was in, we got ready for the big event, with mine and Lila's families all turning up. Hours upon hours went by, with the doctors telling us, "This is most likely going to run into the next day," and after telling most of the family to go home and come back in the morning, Lila gave birth at two-thirty in the morning.

Handing me the baby the doctor said, "Say hello to your daughter."

"Daughter?" I said.

"Yes you have a beautiful baby girl."

Now Lila and me were convinced this baby was a boy, calling it baby Tony all the way through the pregnancy, and I have to say it came as a shock that it was a girl. Holding the baby in my arms I pulled the blanket back from its face to reveal the biggest pair of eyes staring back at me I had ever seen on a child, and my heart melted. Never before had I felt such a true feeling of love as I did in that precise moment. Walking as if on air I carried the baby out of the door of the delivery suit and with a nurse running after me shouting, "You can't take her out, we haven't even checked her over yet."

"She is mine and I can take her where ever I want," came my reply.

Walking into the waiting room to where my father and mother-in-law were waiting, I said, "Say hello to your new granddaughter," and I swear she looked at them and smiled.

Collecting Lila and the baby from the hospital two days later, while traveling home we said, "What are we going to call her?" and came up with the name Lila Tawny, born on the 2nd of April 1984.

Not long after this we returned to Doncaster as my brother John had taken a turn for the worse. Driving him to Leeds Royal Infirmary to get his treatment one day I said, "You have to get a bit better you know, we want to get the baby christened soon. I will have to get out and get us a few quid to buy something nice for us to wear."

"I will try," he said, "I will try."

Making our way to the hospital he looked as if he wanted to tell me something, and turning to me he said, "You know what my mush, you have to stop worrying about money all the time, you're going to worry yourself to death. I would give everything I have in the world and walk down the road naked just to be fit and healthy again, so do me a favor and stop worrying. As long as you can have a nice quality of life and all the things you want, you have them because life is too short not to."

While having his treatment his condition got very bad and they had to admit him into the hospital. Knowing what I know now, I think what he wanted to tell me on the way to Leeds was that he was not going to make it, and say goodbye, but didn't for the sake of my feelings. Moving John into a private room, the doctor came and told us that he did not have long to go, and we should say our goodbyes. My mother, brother Joe and I held his hands and watched as he slipped away. With my mother telling him how much she loved and would always love him he passed away, forever lost to us, forever loved by us. People talk of there being a life after death, and I pray that is the case for I would dearly love to see my brother John again just once, to tell him how much he truly meant to me.

CHAPTER THIRTY

Bringing John home to his trailer, my parents told us children of his wishes to be cremated and his ashes spread into the water off the coast of one of his favorite beaches, saying that he had told them if this disease was to kill him, "Make sure to cremate me because I don't want to be dead and this thing still be alive in side of me." So as per his wishes, he was cremated in Doncaster Rose Hill cemetery. He was 25 years old.

The loss of my brother was nearly to take a second victim, as my mother lost the will to live, saying over and over again, "This is not right, I am not supposed to outlive my children," and I think if not for the sake of her other children and grandchildren she would have took her own life. But life goes on and after some time we managed to resume some form of normality. But to this day, for the reason of it is where my brother died, Doncaster has some significant hold on us all. John never got to be my daughter's godparent, but I would never put anyone in his place, so neither she nor any of my children were baptized.

It took some time but with his words ringing in our ears – "If anything happens to me, don't mourn me, get on and live a happy life" – we set about building our future without him. Moving down to St Ives near Cambridge we pulled onto Ernie Greens camp. By now our full-time work was tarmacking and hot bitumen spray and chippings which we would carry out charging a per-square-meter price, and business was good.

It was during this time I first started working with my wife's uncle Jimmy Frankham, from Red Lodge near Newmarket, who had his own tar tanker and chipping truck. Although much older than me with him having sons older than I, we still got on very well, and as I was to find out in years to come he was more of a man than all of his sons put together. It was while doing a job with Jimmy I was to come across the first mobile phone I had ever seen, after two salesmen approached me asking if my company would be interested in taking some on for our work, showing me a small black box with a phone clipped to the side and the name "Motorola" written on it. Thinking they were kidding I said, "So that is a phone?"

"Yes," they said.

"So I can dial a number into it and it will work like a normal phone?"

"Yes," again came their reply. "Here give it a try," they said handing me the control part.

Dialing my mother and father's home number into it I was amazed when it started ringing the other end. Looking at Jimmy I said, "It's ringing," and you can imagine the look on my face when my father picked up the phone and said, "Hello."

Now this was 1984 and such a thing as a mobile phone was unheard of, telling my father, "You won't believe this but I am talking to you on a phone that is not connected to nothing."

"Really?" he said.

"Yes," I said, like I had just seen a magician do a magic trick, asking the salesmen what did we have to do to get our hands on one. They told us, "All you need is a bank account in any name and we can supply them to you on a three-month contract."

After giving them the details the required they handed two phones to me and Jimmy. "Do you know of anyone else who might like one?" they asked.

Now think about it, a mobile phone was like a gift from God to Gypsies, living in trailers, having to drive to a phone box to make calls. After taking these two salesmen for a cup of coffee we ascertained that it turned out they worked on a commission basis of £400 for every phone they connected, and were willing to split this with us for every customer we could bring along, with a bank account number being all that was required. Now at this time you could walk into any bank and open an account in any name with no ID, so after telling them, "We can sell as many as you can get your hands on," and them taking our new mobile numbers and agreeing to call us later that evening we shook hands and said goodbye.

Within hours of reaching home we had over a hundred orders. Telling everyone to open an account and come along to my place the next day, we spoke to the phone salesmen, who could not believe their luck and said, "What time do you want us there?"

With word of mouth spreading like wildfire, we were to go on and sell hundreds of these phones to other Gypsy people. The phone never stopping ringing, with some people driving down from Scotland picking up as many as they could carry in their cars. This was one of my biggest business mistakes I think I was ever to make, for instead of opening up a proper phone shop we were content just to take a share of the commission and go about our normal business. Especially after the people got used to having the phones, when they got cut off it was as though they had lost an arm, bearing in mind that most of them were now running their business from them. I was to go on and make another small fortune getting them re-connected once switched off. It was only some years later after watching a documentary on the owner and founder of Carphone Warehouse – who it turns out started life as a second-hand car dealer who bought a mobile phone and after attending an auction was inundated with orders from other car dealers to get them one too – that I would realize my mistake. Some Gypsy people like to make the claim that they were the first to own a mobile phone in England, but I can assure you me and Jimmy were the very first.

By now my brother Lee and sisters Nicky and Romain were married, with Lee and Nicky marrying two of our second cousins Jimmy and Michele Taylor, and Romain marrying Jimmy Frankham's son Tommy. I had introduced my sister to him some years earlier after bringing him home with me from Newmarket, from one of my visits there to see Lila who had been stopping on her uncle's place while we were courting. He had fallen out with his father and been thrown out of the family home. He was to stop with us for some months with me taking him out to work, and showing him the ropes of tarmacking. After marrying my sister Romain we were to move back to Doncaster to another camp owned by old friends of my parents, Billy and Flora Adams. It was here we would get arguing while playing a game of football.

Now the Frankhams are relations to Gypsy Johnny Frankham ex-light heavyweight British Champion, and boxing runs in their blood, with Tommy and his two brothers being top amateur boxers having hundreds of fights between them. While rowing with my brother Joe over who could run the furthest turning into who could fight the best, thinking he was not only a friend of mine, but now married to my sister, I would try and calm the situation down, saying, "Leave off now the two of you," only to be told by him, "Don't tell me to leave off."

"Hang on a minute," I said, "I am only trying to stop the two of you fighting."

"I don't give a fuck about fighting you," he said, now switching his attention from my brother to me.

Ripping my shirt off and telling him to put his hands up, I flew into him with all my might, hitting him with shot after shot knocking him to the ground. By now my temper had got the best of me and I went to kick him, only to be stopped by my brother Joe grabbing me by the arm and saying, "You have no need to kick him, give him fair play." (This would be a mistake my brother would live to regret.) Letting him get to his feet he said, "I have had enough," and so the fight was stopped. With my father running over and helping him to his van, he and my sister drove away.

Moving from Doncaster on my own to York in readiness for the fair, my family pulled to a field near Goodwood for to attend the races, along with Romain and Tommy, thinking the argument was finished with – only for Joe and Tommy Frankham to get arguing again. Calling me my brother Joe said, "Tommy has been telling people that you did not beat him when you last fought, and he wants to fight you again."

"OK," I said, "I will be down tonight, tell him to be ready, and tell him this time we fight till it's finished."

Jumping in my Land Cruiser Jeep along with Lila and Lila Tawny we set off for Goodwood. Reaching there in the early evening, I jumped out of my car and said, "Where is he?"

"I am here," he said.

With the men of the camp forming a circle to watch the fight we set to fighting. Now as I have said Tommy was a good boxer, but in a Gypsy fight there is no rest time and no break in between rounds, and this was my kind of fighting.

Seeing that their brother was losing his older brothers Jimmy and Bobby attempted to pull me off of him. As that my brother Joe started fighting with Bobby hitting him and knocking him to the ground. Shouting, "Get up," he allowed him to get to his feet. Concentrating on my own fight with Tommy who was now flagging, he grabbed hold of me and tried to bite me. Saying, "Oh you want it that way do you?" I grabbed him and bit his neck. Shouting for help his brother Jimmy ran in and pulled me off of him, hitting me on the back of my head. With my father now pulling Jimmy away Tommy ran away from me. About a hundred yards away my brother Joe and Bobby Frankham were still fighting. Hitting Joe with a good shot and knocking him down Bobby stepped back to let Joe get back to his feet, but Tommy who had run from me, ran over and kicked Joe in the face, knocking him out and breaking his jaw in two places. Seeing this I ran to my car and pulled a weapon from the back seat, running at the Frankhams who now realizing what they had done, and seeing my father and brother Lee were now armed, ran for their lives. Chasing them they jumped in Jimmy's car and sped off. After seeing that my sister Tawny had got Joe in her car and was taking him to hospital, I jumped into my own car and drove after the Frankhams, knowing they were heading for a hotel where the rest of their family were waiting. I parked my car and made my way into the lobby, walking in; to my surprise the police were already there. Seeing me one of them shouted to the police, "Stop him he has a gun, he is going to shoot us."

Saying, "What are you talking about I don't have no gun," looking at old Jimmy I said, "Have they told you what they did?"

He just nodded his head. I then said, "Don't you think they are in enough trouble without trying to have me locked up?"

Jimmy looked at me and said, "No one is getting locked up here son."

Looking at Tommy I said, "Don't think for a second I didn't see what you did, and you will pay for that I promise."

With him shouting, "What did you say?" in front of the policemen I turned and walked out.

Returning to the camp site to hear the news that Joe's jaw was badly broken and would require surgery to repair it, I could not control my temper. Taking a baseball bat from my car I proceeded to beat Tommy and Romain's trailer to the ground. This is something I regret, for as much as it was his trailer it was hers, and no matter what, she was and is my baby sister.

The next day after my brother came out of hospital, I hooked his trailer on and moved him up to York next to me, going out to work with him as he could not speak properly due to his jaw being wired up. We went about our life as normal, but without saying a word we knew what was on both of our minds: "Payback".

CHAPTER THIRTY-ONE

Within a few weeks Joe's jaw got better, and while coming home from work one day he said, "I think it's time we paid our brother-in-law a visit."

Just nodding my head we drove home, loaded two pump-action shotguns into our car and set off for London. After a phone call to one of Tommy's so-called friends who told us exactly where he was living at that time, we made our way to Cranleigh in Surrey.

Waiting till it got dark, we drove on to the site. What we did not know was that Lila had seen us putting the guns in the car, and putting two and two together she decided to tell my mother what she had seen, who had called my sister Romain to tell her we were on our way. Just as we entered the site out came Tommy trying to make his escape, nearly driving headlong into the front of our car in his panic to get away. With Joe driving up to the front of his car blinding him with the headlights, I jumped from the car, gun in hand. Now blocked in by a car behind and Joe in front, Tommy had nowhere to go. Aiming the gun at the lower part of the door, my intention was to take the leg he had used to kick my brother with, I pulled the trigger, re-loaded and let it go again. Tommy managed somehow to get over to the other side of the car. Thinking, "I haven't hit him yet, better aim a bit higher," as the shot blew out the driver's window he sprang from the car and ran away, running after him while still firing the gun. He made it to some trees and safety. Getting in the car my brother said, "How lucky is that cunt? You put three shots into that car."

"I know," I said, "but his luck will run out one day."

Returning to Doncaster after a stop to drop the guns off at a friend's place, we awoke the next morning to the sound of police cars pulling up outside my father's house. Answering the door my father said, "What do you want?"

"Are you Johnny Marshall?"

"Yes," he replied, "I'm Johnny Marshall."

"Well Johnny I am a Chief Inspector from Suffolk Police, and I have come here to tell you if your sons go anywhere near any of the

Frankhams again, I will lock them up and throw away the keys, understand?"

"Yes I understand," my father said.

Without saying another word the officer turned and walked away. I remember my father saying, "That was a long way to come to make a courtesy call, but take heed of that warning boys."

"Fuck 'em," I said, "he is getting it."

Some time later while driving in the car with my father-in-law John, we were to get stopped for no tax on his car. Thinking I did not have any problems, after giving my name, I was arrested and told I was wanted in Suffolk for attempted murder, but after the police made a call to Suffolk Police I was let go again with the warning stay away from the Frankhams or else. Shortly after this Tommy and Romain, on the advice of my mother who had told them, "The boys won't stop until they get him", left the UK and went to America, with my mother arranging for old family friends, Hamilton Forrest and his family to meet them and look after them while they were there, which they most kindly did, leaving such an impression on Tommy Frankham that his oldest son is called Thomas Hamilton, after our very old family friend.

Some time later me, Lila and my sister Tawny and Bob decided to take another trip Down Under. Selling our cars we boarded a plane bound for Sydney, along with Bob's sister Safire and brother Joe who were still single. Reaching Australia we were met at the airport by my uncle Dids and an old friend of ours from our first visit there, Colin Keeling. Taking us back from the airport I rode in with my uncle, who asked, "What work are you thinking of doing son?"

"Tarmacking," was my reply.

"Well it just so happens I have two tarmac jobs to do Tony and it's far too hot of work for me at my age, so you're more than welcome to them."

Thanking him we made our arrangements for him to pick me up the next day and show me the locations. After doing the two jobs that more than covered our expenses, we set about getting ourselves new trailers and cars. At this time Australia was a gold mine for tarmacking, with every person you spoke to having a use for it: going out hawking (cold calling) in the morning, we would return two hours later having taken seven or eight jobs. At this time we were working a scheme called footage, where you ask a price of so much per square foot: that sounds cheap, but when you measure up it comes to quite a bit of money and business was great.

But it was not long before we run into some problems. After doing a job and having an argument to get paid, the person we were working for went to the police and told them we had threatened him, on this occasion not true, but nonetheless we had a warrant out for our arrests. Deciding that the last place we wanted to be locked up was Down Under, we made the decision to return to the UK. Landing back in London we made our way up to Doncaster, which by now was under six inches of snow, and work was virtually impossible, so after seeing mine and Lila's families to say goodbye again, me, Lila and Lila Tawny returned to Sydney ourselves, thinking we would keep a low profile and continue where I had left off in doing a nice lot of work. Renting a penthouse apartment in Crows Nest, a high-level area of Sydney, I went about my daily duties of going to work.

All was going well, apart from Lila was feeling lonely being alone all day with just the baby for company, so we decided to buy a small trailer and move around a bit. Taking my two workmen with me in a tent, we set out for Western Australia and parts of this massive country we had never seen. Making our way west we would stop off at little camping sites that were dotted along the highway, reaching one in a place called Orange, where we stayed for a couple of weeks, with me going to work in the mornings trying to get finished early so I could come back and take the girls swimming.

Setting off again one afternoon with me towing my trailer and my men behind towing the low loader with the tools on, what started as a pleasant evening's travel would turn into something like out of a horror movie. Now I had spent quite a bit of time in Australia over the years, and had come across my fair share of kangaroos, but what I didn't know is that out in the bush, they make their way onto the roads in the night time to get the warmth from the asphalt, so after one or two near misses with my van, I instructed my men to drive in front and I would follow closely behind. Suddenly out of nowhere jumped a giant of a kangaroo right in front of my workmen's car, now this was no small car, but a Ford Falcon station wagon. Unable to swerve in time my men hit it head on, smashing the front of the car as if they had hit a concrete pole. Pulling to the side, we pushed the car and low loader over to the side of the road to inspect the damage.

As we were looking we heard what sounded like gun shots in the distance, slowly getting closer; then all of a sudden out of the bushes drove a Land Cruiser pick-up with spotlights on the roof shining right into our eyes, blinding us for a moment. As we regained our vision we could see two men, one driving and the other on the back controlling the spotlights. Pulling over to where we were standing the one on the back jumped off and as he walked towards us we noticed he was covered in blood and was holding a high powered rifle. Exiting the driver's seat we could see the other man was equally plastered with blood.

"What's happening here?" said the driver, who as he spoke you could here he was drunk or drugged out of his mind. Looking back towards where Lila and the baby was sitting in my van I gestured for her to lock the doors.

"We hit a roo," said one of my workmen.

"Oh yea," he said, "where is it?"

"It got knocked into that ditch over there," he replied.

Walking over to the ditch this man pulled the kangaroo out by its tail, dragged it over to the side of his truck, then reaching into the back he pulled out a machete and in one swipe took the head clean off the kangaroo. Then as the blood squirted all over him, he picked it up and hooked it onto a hook that hung from the side of his truck.

Then turning back towards us with his eyes bolting out of his head from the rush he had got from the decapitation of the animal, he looked at me and said, "Where are you from?"

"Sydney," I said.

Looking towards my car he said, "Who's in the van?"

"My wife," I replied.

Walking back over to where the driver was standing these two men that looked like something out of *The Texas Chainsaw Massacre*, started whispering to each other. Now this was enough for me, looking at my men I said, "Stay with the car and tools, I will go get someone to tow you in from the next town."

"Please don't leave us," the one said, "not out here with these two fucking nutcases."

Not wanting to run but heading to my van as quick as I could, I jumped in and after telling my men I would be back first thing in the morning, I sped away.

Returning the following morning to where the car was parked, my workmen were nowhere to be seen. I could see that they had lit a fire, but it had long since burned out. Looking around and shouting their names but with no reply, I started to think the worst. Walking back to my van and beeping the horn several times, still nothing, so deciding that I had better go and report them missing I started the van, and just as I was turning around I saw something or someone moving far off in the distance. Stopping the van I could see it was my workmen running towards me, waving their arms. On reaching me they looked scared to death,

"What happened?" I said.

"When you left last night those two men drove away but came back and stopped over there" – pointing to a place in the distance – "and started shooting their guns at us."

"What," I said, "they tried to shoot you?"

"No they were shooting over our heads and laughing, so we ran off into the bush and they chased us in the truck. We hid under some bushes and they were looking for us, saying, 'Come out come out wherever you are.' Tony please get us out of here."

"OK," I said, so hooking a tow rope onto their car I towed them back into the town, where I had left Lila and the baby on a camping site. Pulling up in front of the first garage we came across, "Listen," I said to the boys, "don't tell anyone what happened last night, we don't know who these people were and if we go to the police it may cause us some problems. You're both OK now and we will be out of here just as soon as we can get your car fixed."

They both just nodded in agreement. Asking the mechanic if he could have a look at the car he said, "I can pull the front back out for you, but your radiator is smashed to bits and I don't have a replacement in stock. I can order one but it will take at least two days to get here from Sydney." Not wanting to stay in this place for two hours let alone two days, I asked him if there was anywhere else I might get one; "Well," he said, "Old Scratchy may have one."

"Who?" was my reply.

"Old Scratchy."

Thinking, "Who the fuck is Old Scratchy?"

He continued to tell me of this man who lived in town that collected old cars and parts, giving me directions to Old Scratchy's me and the boys jumped in the van and drove round to his house. Pulling up we could see that he had bits of old cars everywhere: in his drive, on his lawn, with a shed at the back so full it was spilling out into the next-door neighbour's lawn. Seeing that he had an old

Ford Falcon, the boys popped the bonnet and said, "Yes this will fit."

Knocking at the door it was opened by Old Scratchy himself, and I could see where he got his nickname from. He looked as though he had not had a wash in years.

"What do you want?" he said.

Telling him that the garage had sent me, he said, "You a pommy mate?"

"Yes I am from England," I replied.

"Well I ain't got one mate," he said.

"But my boys have said there is one in that old Falcon over there," I said.

Now Old Scratchy was a real Brit-hater, as you come across in Australia from time to time. "Look mate, I have told you I ain't got one, and even if I did I wouldn't sell it to no pommy," came his reply.

Before I could answer I heard a woman's voice from inside the house say, "Sell 'em the bloody part you old bugger."

"Shut up you," said Old Scratchy.

"I said sell 'em the bloody part," said the voice again, and out of the house stepped an Aborigine woman who could hardly fit through the door. "Take no notice of him," she said, "he can be a grumpy old bugger sometimes, and I should know, I have been with him for long enough." Looking at me she said, "You from London?"

"Yes," I said.

"Do you know the Queen?" she asked.

"Sorry," I said.

"Well if you live in London you must know the Queen. If I get him to sell you the part you want will you do me a favor, will you get the Queen to send me a letter?"

Thinking, "My God where am I?" – just because I said I live in England does not mean I know the Queen, but I suppose her small-town mentality was that she knew everyone for miles around and we must be the same. Wanting to get the radiator and get out of there as quick as I could, I said, "Of course I will, just as soon as I get home."

"OK," she said, "thanks."

Looking at him she said, "Go get your tools and take the part off and let them have it for free."

"Oh no," I said, "I don't want it for free, I will pay you whatever you want for it and my boys will remove it, so as not to give you any work or put you out in any way."

Agreeing on a price my boys took the part off and away we went. Reaching the garage and after asking the mechanic to fit it straightaway, once again I heard this woman's voice, turning to see her and Old Scratchy coming out of the off-license across the road carrying a large crate of beers that had obviously been bought with the money I had paid them for the radiator. "Yoo-hoo!" she shouted, "don't forget to speak to the Queen."

Thinking to myself, "This place is like an outdoor mental asylum," we got the car running and after a quick stop to pick up my trailer, off we went as fast as we could.

CHAPTER THIRTY-TWO

Reaching the town of Wagga Wagga where I had stopped as a young man for the Christmas of 1978 with my family, we pulled onto a nice camp and the next day off I went hawking (calling for work). Taking a big job in a wood factory to start the following morning, next day bright and early I took the men to the job. While they were cleaning and preparing it I went to get us some breakfast; returning shortly after I noticed my men were nowhere to be seen. Thinking "Something is wrong", I turned to leave when up pulled a police car blocking my path, then another and another. Opening my window to ask what the problem was, I was pulled from the vehicle and thrown to the floor. After being handcuffed and told I was under arrest, they threw me into the back of one of the cars and took me to the police station. On arriving I said, "Do you mind if someone could please tell me what the hell is going on? I am a tourist in this country and I demand to know why I am being treated in this manner."

Well, it turned out that some other Englishmen had been there some weeks before doing tarmac work and caused a lot of problems, overcharging for their work and demanding to be paid, and the police had run an advert in the local paper asking anyone who gets approached to have any work done to contact them. Telling them I had only came along for the day after meeting some other British men on the camping site the night before, just to lend a hand, they said, "We will see about that mate," and locked me in a cell.

Returning some hours later, they said, "You have a visitor." Bringing me into a visit room there was Lila, who after I had not came home knew something was up and contacted the local police station who told her I was there. Holding Lila Tawny I told her, "It's all right, just a misunderstanding and I will be out in a little while."

As we were talking in walked an officer and said, "You came from Sydney to here, right, Mr Marshall?"

"Yes," I replied.

"Well it seems there's a warrant for your arrest in Sydney, for some work you did and the CID from there are coming over to collect you."

Looking at Lila I said, "You have to go, get to Sydney and go to my uncle Dids, tell him I said to put you on a plane home to your Mum and Dad."

"I can't leave you," she said.

"Listen to me just do as I ask, if this is what I think it is we will lose everything. Now go to the trailer, get the money and anything else you need and go."

At this time Lila was still only 20 years old and expecting our second child and had never been anywhere on her own. Starting to cry she said, "But I can't just leave you here, and I don't even have your uncle's number."

"Go to a hotel, call my father. He will speak to them and tell them to come get you. Don't worry, you will be alright."

Kissing her and the baby goodbye, I sent them on their way, then sat down and put my mind to how I was going to get out of this mess. Asking to speak to one of the officers I said, "Listen, Sir, there must be some mistake here; you say I am wanted in Sydney for work that was done some months back. How can this be me when I only came into the country six weeks ago? You can check with customs and they will confirm what I am telling you is the truth," thinking this will not work as they must be smart enough to ask if I had been in and out, and how many times in the last year, but it was worth a shot as I had nothing to lose. When to my surprise, back came the officer and said, "Well mate we have spoken to the customs and you're telling the truth, you did only fly in a few weeks ago, and if you can follow me, we are letting you go."

Leaving the police station I knew it was only a matter of time before they realized their mistake and would be coming for me again, so pulling up at the first phone box I called my father asking where Lila was and telling him what had happened,

"Get out of there now," was his advice. "Don't worry about that," I said, "I will be on the next plane."

Reaching the hotel where Lila had gone to, the look on her face when she opened the door was a picture. Quickly telling her the story, I looked at my workmen who had been released the same time as me. "OK listen boys, this is what I need you to do. Take my van and leave your car with me, go back to the camp and hook my trailer on, you know how to unhook the electric cable and put the jacks up, because you have done it enough times with me."

"But Tony," the one said, "we have never towed anything as big as your caravan before."

"Listen you will be alright, just take your time and it will be fine, I will be waiting on you along the road out of town. When you see me just follow me to where we are going."

"OK," they said and off they went.

As they left, me, Lila and the baby jumped in the old work car and headed out of town. Pulling into a McDonalds car park we got some food and waited. After a while down the road came the boys flying, with my trailer on the back. Shooting out in front of them they flashed the lights to let me know they had seen me. Knowing a man in a place about one hundred miles away called Cowra who my father had sold trailers to in the past would be a buyer for my van and trailer, we made our way there. By now it was dark and every mile we traveled I felt more and more relaxed, thinking it was one more mile of distance between me and the law.

Coming through a small town I saw a police car and as we passed by it pulled out behind the boys in the van. Checking my rear-view mirror I saw another police car drop in behind; thinking, "That's it the ghost is up," when all of a sudden on came their lights. Overtaking the trailer and van they shot in front of them and blocked the road between them and me in the old Ford Falcon. Still looking in the mirror I heard Lila shout, "Stop!" Looking up there was a train signal crossing coming down right in front of me; slamming my breaks on I stopped just in time. Looking around I could see that the police had stopped the boys in the van and had them out and over the front of a car, handcuffing them. Now anyone who has ever been to Australia will tell you the trains out in the bush go on for miles, but this one seemed as though it was never-ending, and the few minutes we waited for it to pass seemed like an eternity, thinking in a minute one of the boys is going to say, "Hey hold on a minute it's not us you want, but him," pointing to me in the work car.

Finally up came the barrier and away we sped as fast as the old car would go. Now remember we just had the radiator replaced and it was not connected properly, so making it to about five miles from Cowra, the steam and water shot out of the bonnet and she blew up. Now it's two o'clock in the morning, and after our last little episode in the bush with crazed gunmen, I was not about to take my wife and baby girl out into the dark, so telling Lila to steer the car with Lila Tawny sleeping in the back I pushed the car the remainder of the way, thinking the whole time, "My God what can go wrong next?" and "Please just let me get my wife and baby home safely." Getting to about half a mile from the town we came to a bit of a hill so running along and jumping in we cruised down the hill and into Cowra. Stopping in front of a hotel we walked in. Telling the hotel clerk we had broken down and that someone would be along later to collect the car, I asked if there was an airport in town with flights to Sydney. "Yes," he said, "but there is only one flight at six in the morning. My wife drives a taxi," he said; "if you like I can have her pick you up at five-thirty. That will give you enough time to catch the plane."

Thanking him we made our way to one of the rooms. Not even taking our clothes off we cuddled in on top of the bed and fell asleep, waking up with a start because the phone was ringing. I answered it. On the other end of the line was the hotel clerk: "I am so sorry I forgot to ring you, it is nearly six, and my wife's waiting for you outside. I have called the airport: they are going to try and hold the plane, but you better hurry."

Knowing that if I did not get out of there immediately the police would put a stop on me traveling out of the country, we raced out the hotel and into the waiting taxi. Pulling right onto the bush runway we boarded what I can only describe as the smallest plane I have ever been on: six seats for passengers and the pilot up front. I will always remember the pilot speaking to us on the intercom when he was so close he could have just talked and we would have heard him; like he was the captain of a 747 jumbo jet.

Landing at Sydney airport we made our way to the British Airways desk, telling them we had a death in the family and needed to return the UK. On checking the lady came back to us and said, "I am so sorry we don't have any seats available until next week."

Now I knew that would be too late and chances were if we did not fly today, we might not get out at all, so after speaking to a supervisor and telling him that my brother had died – thinking, well my brother had died and I was sure John wouldn't mind me using his name to make my escape – he agreed to put us on emergency standby with all the airlines, telling us to come back in one hour and he would see what he could do, but that if he could get us on we might not be sitting together. Telling him, "My friend, I don't care if you have to strap me to the wing, just get us home please."

Returning one hour later the same supervisor came and met us saying, "I have some good news for you. I have you on the 3 o'clock flight to Heathrow. You're in separate parts of the plane but I have sent word to the cabin crew to get you together once on board."

Thanking him we got our boarding passes and went to get me a change of clothes as I was still wearing my work clothes. Waiting for the plane to be called we kept out of sight, sitting in a play area for the baby. Thinking they should have called this flight by now I went back over to the check in desk to ask why.

The man who had sorted the seats out saw me and said, "What are you still doing here?"

"I have been waiting for them to call our flight number," I said.

"But this is the domestic departure lounge, not the international," came his reply, "and if I am not mistaken that flight has left."

CHAPTER THIRTY THREE

Seeing the look on my face, the poor man looked as if he was going to cry himself as I tried to explain that my brain was not working right, because of all the stress I was under. Running to the phone he called up and got the plane that by now had left the docking area and was on its way to the run way to turn around.

Telling us the directions to the gate in the other side of the airport he said, "Good luck fella, now run."

With the baby in my arms and Lila carrying the bag with everything we had in the world inside, we ran through the airport as if our lives depended on it, with "Will Mr and Mrs Marshall please make your way to gate number 43 immediately" ringing in our ears over the airport intercom, thinking, "I wish they would stop saying our names over and over again for everyone to hear, including the police". Turning a corner I ran straight into four policemen, nearly knocking them to the ground. "You must be Mr and Mrs Marshall," one of them said, thinking after all that they still caught me, only for them to laugh and say, "Well you better hurry up, they won't hold that plane for much longer."

Standing like a rabbit in the headlights it took me a second to realize they were not there for me, but just passing through the same part of the airport. We set off running again, getting to the plane that by now was well delayed because of us. With the other passengers looking at us like devils we took off, bound for London.

For the next 24 hours we sat and talked about "What if they are waiting for us when we land?" "Well," I said, "there's nothing we can do about it, we will have to just wait and see."

Landing, we cleared customs and made our way outside and into the arms of Lila's mother and father John and Zenda Doe. Handing them the baby I felt like I could kiss the ground, I was so glad to be home.

That day I phoned Bob from Caravan City, Cowra, whom I had been making my way to for to sell my trailer and van, telling him the whole score of what had happened and asking him to get a solicitor in to my work boys. Bob said, "I can do better than that. Fax me a letter to act on your behalf, saying that the caravan was being delivered to me, and I will go to the police station myself to see what can be done. Give me a call this time tomorrow and I will let you know."

Thinking, "Well I have nothing to lose," I went to an office and sent him the letter, calling him the next day. Bob came on the phone and said, "I have some good news for you son, your van and trailer are here in my yard, and I got the two boys out. They are in one of my trucks on the way back to Sydney. Now how much do you want for the van and trailer?"

Now I am in England and this man has a letter in his hand saying he has already paid for these items. "Bob, I will leave it completely up to you," I said, thinking that anything is better than nothing.

"No son," he said, "you should know me better than that, how much did you pay for the trailer?"

Telling him the price he said: "I will give you your money back for that, and the van," he said, "I will pay you so much for." Again this was almost as much as I had given for it.

"Bob," I said, "you are a gentleman."

"Never mind that," he said, "Send me your account number and say hello to your old Dad for me will ya?"

Thanking him again I put the phone down, and the next day I sent him my account details and the best bottle of Scotch I could find.

Returning back to my parents who were now living in the bungalow in front of the camp at Tilts Farm in Doncaster, where my trailer was left, we set about getting our lives back together. After buying a transit van, we pulled down to Lila's Mum and Dad's at a place called Cleeve Prior, near Evesham in Worcestershire. This was a piece of land my father-in-law had bought many years before, and had become like a second home to us.

Settling down to work with Lila booked into the local hospital to have the baby we decided to find out the sex of the baby. Attending the scan the nurse said, "It's a girl."

Now I love my children with all my heart, but I would be telling a lie if I did not admit I wanted a son, desperately. Our second daughter Montana was born on the 10th of November 1987 in Reditch: she was beautiful, weighing 8lb 9oz. Within two months Lila was expecting again. Coming home from work one day she came running out of the trailer smiling at me. "Guess what?" she said. "We are having twins."

"Oh that's cushty (good)," I said, "one of them has to be a boy."

Seven months later she gave birth to identical baby girls. We named them Amber and Jade. Our two precious gems.

With four kids all under the age of four Lila had a lot on her hands, but I helped as much as I could with night feeds and such. Now I know I have said I wanted a boy, but every time my girls were born and put into my arms, I fell madly in love with them at first glance, and would not have changed them for all the sons in the world. They are and always will be my most valued treasures, and have grown into the most beautiful and loving people I know.

Moving back to Doncaster to spend some time with my parents, we attended a fancy dress Christmas party my sister Tawny was having in the local night club, "Seventh Heaven". During the night I saw some boys having words with my father, who was dressed as J. R. Ewing from the big show on television at that time, "Dallas". Seeing this, I walked over and said, "What's wrong Dad?"

"Oh nothing," he said, "just some silly little cunt thinking he was being cheeky asking me where my horse was."

Looking at these young men, I asked who was cheeky to my father. With no reply I said, "Do any of you want to be cheeky to me?"

"No we didn't mean no harm," said one of them, "we were only having a laugh."

"Well, my father is not a person you want to have a laugh at, now fuck off over there and behave yourselves."

During my time in Australia my brother Joe had forgave Tommy Frankham, after sending my sister Romain to see him asking if what had happened could please be forgot and forgiven. But I was still not speaking, as anyone who knows me will testify I have a problem with forgive and forget. Coming to me one day my brother Joe said, "I want to ask you a favour."

"What?" I said.

"I want you to speak to Tommy and Romain. I have forgave it for the sake of my sister and I want you to do the same."

Leaving he returned some time later with Tommy and asked us to shake hands. Deciding to let it go we shook hands and I never mentioned it again.

Later that week my sister was having another party at which Tommy and Romain were invited. Turning up he said, "Me and you are going to get very drunk tonight and have a great night just like old times," and it was like old times: laughing and dancing, we were all having a wonderful time, when all of a sudden two girls got fighting on the dance floor right next to us. Seeing this I said, "Oh don't do that girls, don't spoil a good night," then out of the corner of my eye I saw the same men I had told off the party before, heading in my direction. Thinking, "Oh shit I am too drunk for this," but turning to face them anyway, without saying a word, me and the oldest one of them set to fighting, trading blow for blow. Now as drunk as I was I was doing OK then out of nowhere this man's brother ran forward with a large glass ashtray and smashed me right in the face with it, knocking me over a table. Rising to my feet, by now my brothers and brothers-in-law were all on the scene. Seeing they were outnumbered these men ran out of the club.

Getting home and looking in the mirror at the damage, I could see they had knocked three of my front teeth out, and cut my lip quite badly inside. After a few phone calls asking who they were, I was told they were the Smiths from Barnsley in Yorkshire, a well-known Gypsy fighting family. After having a bridge fitted to replace my teeth, I set about the task of getting myself fit, knowing that a rematch was on the cards with these men who had given me such a bad beating. It was some months later while attending a party in York I was to come across the elder brother of my two attackers, stepping from my car with my brother-in-law, he said, "There is your man."

Looking over I could see he was buying his ticket so as to gain entry into the party. Walking over I put my hand into my pocket and slipped on a knuckle-duster, thinking, "The last thing I am giving you is fair play after your treatment of me last time." Seeing me coming he attempted to walk by me; as he reached my location, without saying a word, I drew off and hit him as hard as I could.

Trying to duck out of the way, the first shot hit him square in the forehead, breaking the knuckle-duster in half, and sending him flying across the front of a car, cutting him quite badly, following up with two or three shots more.

This young man's fighting instinct kicked in. Knowing if he went down he would most probably not be getting back up, he grabbed hold of me trying to get his head back together, but with me not about to allow this to happen I continued to hit him with shot after shot. Now this man was one of the strongest men I had ever come across, as I had hit him with everything but the kitchen sink and he still would not go down. Grabbing him round the neck I took the end of the broken knuckle duster that was sticking out of my hand like a knife and proceeded to stab it into his head and face. With the blood now spraying out everywhere he dropped to his knees, stepping back I ran and kicked him as hard as I could, sending him straight over the bonnet of a car. To my amazement he landed on his feet the other side and ran away down the road.

Leaving the club we returned home to my father's thinking, "They will be back for revenge." We had not been there long when the phone rang. It was this boy's father asking to speak to mine, saying, "Johnny this is going to end up with one of these boys dead and the other doing life in prison, if we don't stop it now. My boy has told me that all your sons were there, but only one fought with him and as far as I am concerned if you agree that's the end of it, your boy got hurt and so did mine, let's leave it at that."

"I don't have a problem with that," said my father, "but let me just tell you this, if one of my boys bump into any of you and you so much as look the wrong way at him, there will be no accounting for what I do."

"Fair enough, that's fair enough," said this man.

Some time later I was to hear that the man I fought was to have 70 stitches in his face and head. Now I have to give credit where credit is due, it would have been all too easy for him to go back and tell his family that we had all set about him, but not only was he one of the strongest men I have ever encountered but one of the straightest.

CHAPTER THIRTY-FOUR

Carrying on with life as normal, with me and Tommy Frankham becoming once again firm friends, working and moving about the country together, spending a summer together down in Devon, and Somerset with Bob and Tawny and our old friends Billy and Jane Dale, stopping at places like Glastonbury, Redruth, and Land's End, it was during our stay at Glastonbury we were to get a call telling us that our brother-in-law Jim Brazil had been involved in a bad car crash and was taken to hospital with serious head injuries

Leaving our four girls with my sister Tawny, me and Lila made our way to Gloucestershire, to be with Lila's sister Lucy who had married Jim a few years earlier and was expecting their third child, having already given birth to two children Jim Jr and baby Lucy. After being taken from Gloucester to Bristol and Frenchay hospital that deals with brain injuries, Jim was to sadly lose his brave fight for life. He was not only my brother-in-law but a most valued friend, and is sadly missed.

After the death of Jim we moved back to be alongside Lucy and the kids, who were now living at her mother and father's in Cleeve Prior. Still working with Tommy tarmacking we were to set off on a course that would see us get in a lot of trouble some years later.

At this time we were setting up companies in fictitious names and asking untold amounts of money per square meter, then demanding to be paid cash, getting caught up in it all and losing our sense of perspective. The money this work generated was phenomenal, but as I have said in the past all things must come to an end. While doing a job one day and waiting to be paid in the man's office, the door was to come crashing open and in rushed a gang of plainclothes policemen. Looking at me the one said, "You're nicked sunshine."

Laughing, I said, "You have been watching too much of 'The Bill' mate," "The Bill" being a well-known television program that came on regularly at that time, in which one of the main characters, DI Burns, would say at least once in every episode, "You're nicked sunshine."

Not taking too kindly to my comment this officer threw me over the desk and put the handcuffs on me, saying, "So you think you're a clever cunt eh? We will see." Taking us to the police station where we were charged, and kept overnight, then sent to Canterbury prison, within a couple of days we were bailed. Turning up one day to a pleas and directions hearing, I noticed that there was an awful lot of extra police on hand in the courthouse.

Turning to my father-in-law who had drove us to the court I said, "I think we are going to be lifted (arrested) again here today John," with him saying "I think you're right son, I have never seen so many gavvers (police) in a court in my life."

Unfortunately I was right: soon as the hearing finished, in walked two plainclothes officers with about twenty in uniform. Walking over to us in the dock, they said, "Antony Marshall and Thomas Frankham, we are Detectives Cornish and Cridland, we are placing you under arrest for crimes committed in the county of Hampshire dating back over the last eight years. We will be taking you to the local police station until such time as we can arrange transportation to take you to Basingstoke for questioning."

Removing us from the dock, one looked at me and said, "We meet at last Mr. Marshall. I have been on your trail for a very long time, and it is a pleasure to finally catch up."

"I am sorry to say I don't feel the same way," was my reply.

Taking us that evening to Basingstoke police station, we were placed in cells for the night and told they would be starting our interviews the following morning. Next day one by one we were taken in to be questioned, telling us that Hampshire police had in fact two taskforce teams set up with the sole purpose of apprehending us – one called Operation Dupe the other operation Onyx – and that they had just missed us on several occasions, whilst cashing cheques in banks over the years. After days of questioning with us both making "no comment" interviews, we came up for a bail application. Although strongly opposed by the prosecution, we were granted bail with very heavy terms, one being that we were to attend the police station in Evesham to sign on three times a day, and were not allowed to enter the county of Hampshire, Kent or Essex for fear we might tamper with witnesses.

Leaving court we made our way home. By now I was living on a piece of land I had bought in Coventry, putting a new twin unit mobile home on it, at a place called Ryton-on-Dunsmore. A group of us had purchased this land for the purpose of developing it into a residential Gypsy camping site. Along with us on the site was my wife's uncle Roy Dunn, his wife Louise and daughter Debby and several other Gypsy families. Lila's mother Zenda is of the Dunn (Lee) family, a very old and well renowned family from North London, with her brothers being well respected Gypsy fighting men of their time, with the eldest brother Tucker being acclaimed as the best man among Gypsies, and the youngest of the four, Ivan, going on to be one of the most noted of North London villains of his time; sadly he was found murdered in a lay-by just off the M25 motorway in Hertfordshire, with his murderers never to be identified. These men although much older than me, were to become some of my closest friends, with Tucker telling me one day, when I could have only been twenty-six years old, that as he was estranged from his family and had been for many years his concern was if he died he would have no one to bury him. "Listen," I said, "I hope you go on to live another 50 years, but whenever it happens, be it a week from now or 50 years, I will bury you and give you the best send-off I can."

"Do you mean that?" he said.

"I wouldn't say it if I didn't mean it," I replied.

Shaking my hand, all he said was "Thank you." Sadly, some years later the day arrived and I kept my promise to Tucker, with his instructions to me carried out to his wishes, and I considered it a great honor to do so.

During my time spent on bail and going over the court documents of statements and such, I was to be introduced to my barrister, by the name of Michael Borelli QC, in my opinion the best legal advocate in the UK. It was during our first meeting he was to look at me and say, "Mr. Marshall I am going to ask you some questions and I would appreciate your honest answers, but first is there anything you would like to ask of me?"

"Well," I said, "first of all, please call me Tony; second, I will answer everything you ask me as honestly as I can, but I want the same respect. To put it bluntly I don't want no barrister bullshit, just the truth as you see it."

"OK Tony," he said, "that is quite fair, and please call me Michael."

Going over the case and the points he needed some clarification on, eventually he was finished: "Now what questions do you have for me Tony?" he asked.

"Only one," I said: "in your expert opinion after going over all the evidence, how long do you think I am going to get in prison?"

Well he said we have an agreement to tell it as we see it, and in my professional opinion, you will be sentenced to 5 years, 4 if we are lucky.

This meeting took place on the 17th of November, my Birthday. "Happy Birthday."

CHAPTER THIRTY-FIVE

For two years and eleven months we waited for the case to come to a conclusion, with us both under the advice of our barristers pleading guilty at the first given opportunity, three months before the final hearing and sentence date.

With me and Lila's 10th wedding anniversary coming up, I decided to take her to New York as I knew I was going away for some years and wanted one last chance before doing so to spend some quality time together. It was my intention to take her to the diamond market in New York and buy her a ring to celebrate our 10 years of marriage. Booking the flights separately with me booking in on my passport in the name of Nelson and Lila booking in her own name, we boarded a flight at Heathrow to New York, staying in the Plaza Hotel.

We spent an amazing five days, going to see Barbra Streisand in Madison Square Garden, taking her on a carriage ride to eat at The Inn on the Green, in Central Park, and shopping in Bloomingdales on 5th Avenue. It was a perfect way to spend some of our last time together, but soon it was over and we had to come home to face the music.

Arriving back in Heathrow and telling Lila to walk ahead of me just in case, we came to customs. As we came around the corner I saw about ten customs officers, and every one of them turned to look at me. Thinking, "This is not right," but hoping that Lila would make it through, they waited till we just about made it to the outer doors before one of them shouted, "Excuse me…"

Making out as if they were talking to someone else, I carried on walking, then as the doors opened in stepped two more officers blocking my path: "Excuse me, Sir, do you mind if we have a word?"

"Why?" I said. "I have people waiting for me outside."

"Well I am afraid they are just going to have to wait," one replied. Taking me to one side they said, "Can we see your passport please?"

"Yes of course," I said.

"Do you mind if we ask you the purpose of your visit to New York?"

"Business." I replied.

"Diamond business?" said one of the officers.

"No I am not in the diamond business," I replied.

"Really?" he said. "So you have not been in New York to buy your wife a ten carat diamond ring, then?"

Just as this, a plainclothes customs officer came into the room, walked over to me and said, "My name is Chief Inspector Khan, Head of Customs here in the airport. I believe you to not be the person your passport pertains to be, and I am placing you under arrest for this and also the reason we believe you may be carrying goods that you are bringing into the country without declaring for duty and excise."

Now luckily I had not bought Lila a ring, and the only thing we were carrying were a few gifts for my girls, but the information these customs men were in receipt of was pretty precise to say the least.

My mind wandered back all those years to when we first returned to the States, and how my father must have felt knowing that someone close had betrayed him, as it was only one or two very close family members who even knew I was traveling.

Taking us into a room I was amazed to see sitting there, one of the detectives from my case. "What are you doing here?" I asked.

"Oh I was just passing by," he said, "just passing by from Basingstoke to Heathrow."

Yeah, right.

After being searched thoroughly, the decision was made to release Lila, but I was to be held and taken to court for traveling outside the country while on bail, so the next morning I was taken up in front of the local magistrates, and remanded to custody, being moved later that day to Wormwood Scrubs Prison in London. Now I had been in prison before but this was a shock, for at this time it was mostly filled with immigration detainees, looking and sounding like something out of the movie *Midnight Express*. Spending three days there I was pleased when they came and told me I was being moved to Winchester Prison in Hampshire, as the court I was to attend for sentencing was in Portsmouth. On reaching Winchester I was placed in a cell with two other young men, who as soon as the door was locked for the night started smoking what is called in prison a "bucket": this is a form of self-made bong. After kindly refusing their offer to share in their bucket, as at this time I didn't even smoke a cigarette, I woke up the next morning smelling like a smoked fish, going to the head screw (top officer) I asked, "Is it possible I can be moved from the cell I am in, as the guys smoke fags and I don't?"

"The only cell we have spare," he said, "is the single medical cell, but you can only get this if you have a medical condition."

"Well," I said, "it just so happens I have asthma."

"Well if that's the case go and see the doctor. If he gives you permission it's all yours."

Putting in an application to see the doctor, I walked into his office. "What can I do for you Mr. Marshall?" he said.

Starting to go into the story of I had chronic asthma, he said, "Stop. What do you want?"

"I want to go into the single cell to stop people smoking all over me," I said.

"Well why didn't you just say that? Take this note to the officers, and tell them I have gave you permission. Now anything else? No? Then goodbye."

Thinking, "What an ignorant bastard" I walked out, but knowing what I know now, this man had to be this way, for all the requests he had to field in a day from the junkies asking for more medication, the likes of methadone and such, for in prison if there are ten men, eight will have some form of drugs habit or another.

Moving into the single cell that was brand new and never been used before, still having the plastic coating on the stainless steel sink and toilet, I felt much better, as for now this was to be my home, and coming from my background of cleanliness, I could not have carried on living with these other men with their way of lives. So after getting a new mop and cleaning products from the stores, I set about cleaning my cell, not stopping till it gleamed like a new penny. When I was finished the screws brought one of the governors along to see it, with him saying, "Now this is how a cell should be cleaned. Would you be interested in being the head wing cleaner, son?"

"No thanks," I replied, "I am hoping to get a job in the gym," as each evening the gym screws would come along the wings asking if anyone wanted to go to the gym and I would always be banging on the door asking to go, and after speaking to the Gym PO I was given the job of "No. 1 Gym Orderly", which suited me down to the ground as one of the things I had told myself was if I am going to do prison time, I would use it wisely and at the same time get myself as fit as I could.

Within a couple of days I was taken to Portsmouth, in front of the judge who was presiding over our case, who remanded me in custody as a flight risk, which was stupid as when they arrested me I was returning back to the UK, not the other way round. I had no intention of running away, as me and Lila had discussed the prospect and came up with the conclusion that if we ran we would have to for the rest of our lives, leaving behind our families and friends, bringing our children up in a foreign country, not able to see their grandparents. So not turning up at court was the last thing on my mind: I had resigned myself to the fact that I was going to do my time and get out, then carry on with the rest of our lives together, to pay my dues so to speak. That week I had my first visit from Lila who I had not seen since the airport, as they would not allow her to see me in Wormwood Scrubs as they said I was only in transit to another prison. She had come along with her uncle Roy Dunn who had drove her down from Coventry, Uncle Roy asking if there was anything I needed done as I had been taken in before I had expected to be, and that if there was anything I needed or wanted done, I only had to ask. This kind gesture is something I will never forget, but he is a man that in his day had served a prison sentence and knows what it is all about, as when you are in prison you soon find out who your real true friends are. As the old saying goes, "a friend in need". Leaving us to talk on our own Uncle Roy said his goodbyes, saying, "Remember if you need anything, you know where I am," and left to wait outside.

Looking at me Lila said, "I knew you could do this, but the way you are handling it makes me feel really proud of you. Do not worry about me or the girls, we will be OK, I promise."

Looking at each other we knew that we were going to get through this no matter what. Kissing her goodbye she said, "I will write to you every day, and never miss a visit, I love you with all my heart and just want to tell you that once again."

Now anyone who has ever been to prison will tell you, the hardest thing about it is being away from those you care about and the feeling of helplessness you feel not being there for them, but apart from that it is like being in school with very strict teachers. You have probably heard the expression that prison is a college for criminals and to a very big degree that is what it is, with the majority of prisoners being in for petty crimes, but some of the men I was to meet and befriend were from the highest ranks of the criminal underworld.

CHAPTER THIRTY-SIX

After serving three and a half months on remand, finally the day arrived to attend court for sentencing. Loading me onto a bus with my hands handcuffed to two screws I noticed that there was armed police on board. Asking one of my escort screws, "What's that all about?", he whispered to me they have had a report that there might be trouble being as I was from a large Gypsy family. "What a waste of taxpayers' money," I thought to myself, shaking my head

Reaching court and being brought up into the dock I was joined by my co-defendants, Tommy Frankham, Edward James, and my cousins John and Gavin Kennedy. With us all pleading guilty at earlier hearings, it was just the mitigating circumstances from our defense barristers that was being heard, and after two days of this the moment came for the judge to give his ruling and pass out his sentence. Asking us to rise he sentenced me to four years, Tommy to three and half years, John to three years, with Edward and Gavin receiving lesser sentences. Jumping to his feet my barrister Michael Borelli demanded that the judge rethink his sentence handed down to me, and after one hour of further deliberations, the judge rescinded and reduced my sentence by one month.

I remember thinking, "Big deal! One month, was that really worth all of the arguing between the judge and my defense for one month?" But what I did not understand at that time was that a sentence of four years and over comes under the Parole Act, whereas three years eleven months, to which I was now sentenced, does not, meaning that after serving half of my time I would be automatically released. This as it turns out was a godsend, for I would never have made parole, and would probably have ended up serving the whole four years. After sentencing, Michael came to see me in the holding cells, telling me, "If you remember, Tony, our conversation when we first met, I said if we get a four we have done really well, so to get it under that and removing the parole aspect, I would hope you are happy."

"Well, Michael, I would be a fool to say I am happy, as I am returning back to prison for the next two years, but I do know how hard you have worked on my behalf during this whole affair, and I would like to truly thank you for that."

Shaking his hand we said our goodbyes, but this would not be the last time I would meet Michael Borelli.

Now convicted, we were all loaded onto the bus and taken back to Winchester Prison. Coming into the reception area, I was greeted by another Gypsy man who I had befriended who worked there. Asking how I got on, telling him of my sentence he said, "Result!"

"Yes," I said, "I think so." knowing we were all going to be sentenced I had already set a plan in action to have a laugh with my co-defendants, having the traveling boy give them all clothes that did not fit them. With my cousin John being about twenty stone and having about a 40 waist the boy gave him a pair of jeans and a T-shirt that would not fit a man half his size; trying to get them on, with me saying, "You have to put on what they give you, or you can lose days."

We watched as he struggled to get them on, managing to get the T-shirt on, only just, and in trying to pull the jeans on he flipped, throwing the jeans at the boy and saying, "I don't give a fuck how many days they give me, they won't fucking fit!"

This was just what was needed to lighten up the mood from the feeling of sadness that I knew they were feeling as everyone does when first coming into prison. After all being allocated their cells I made sure that the gym screws got them out and brought them down to the gym, so they could spend as much time out of their cells as possible, and as I had spent some months now in prison, I wanted to make them aware of the do's and don'ts of prison life, but within a few weeks we were all sent our separate ways, with John, Gavin and Edward all going up north so as they would be closer to their families, Tommy being sent to High Down, and me being allocated to transfer to a prison called Coldingly near Woking in Surrey.

Now as prisons go Winchester was not so bad and I had it pretty easy, what with being the No. 1 Gym Orderly. All I had to do was make sure the boys who worked with me kept everything clean and tidy, once a day dropping the dirty laundry off in the morning and collect the clean. Making sure everything was done first thing in the morning gave me the full day to myself, which I spent training, taking part in all of the activities like football, basketball, handball, and of course the circuits and weight training three times a day. I had never been so fit in my life, but even though I asked if I could carry out the remainder of my sentence there, I was told I had to move on and move on I did.

Two days before I was due to leave, while waiting for my door to be opened at 7 am, there was an eerie silence fell over the place, 7 am came and went, and seeing one of the screws passing my door, I asked, "What's going on Gov?" ("Gov" being what an inmate calls a prison officer in the south of England and up north they call them "Boss".)

"No work today, Marshall."

"Why?" I asked.

"Someone has hung himself on the Remand Wing, and no one is allowed out until the police do their investigations."

Never before had I heard the prison so quiet, and it brought back memories of my father telling me the story of being in Wandsworth prison in 1953 when they hung Derek Bentley for the murder of a police officer in London, and of how you could hear a pin drop. I think the reason for this silence in my case, is it makes you think what could cause someone to take their own life, and will I be strong enough to cope with what I have to do and make it out of these walls.

Arriving at Coldingly Prison, I was booked in and taken to a wing, this was late November and freezing outside. Reaching the cell, the screw opened the door, and as I walked in I could see that the person who had been living in this cell before me had obviously went berserk and smashed it to bits; the chair, table and even the window was smashed. Stepping back out I said, "I am not going in there."

"Why?" he said. "I know it is a bit rough but we can try and get you a new chair and stuff."

Looking at him I said, "A bit rough? I would not put a dog in that cell, and for sure I will not be going in it."

"Well it is the only cell we have available at the minute so you will have to make do for this evening, and we will try and sort something out tomorrow morning."

"Listen," I said, "I don't think you understand, I am not living in there for one minute, never mind one night."

"Well if you won't go in I am going to have to nick you (put you on report)."

Now losing my temper, I said, "Do you think I give a fuck about being nicked? I may be a prisoner under your control, but you don't fucking own me, do you understand?"

Hearing this commotion, another inmate came walking over. Shaking my hand he said, "Alright brov, my name is Keith." Looking inside the cell then back towards the screw he said, "Come on, Gov, no wonder the geezer don't want to go in this cell, would you sleep in there?"

"It doesn't matter where I would sleep," he said, "I am not a prisoner."

"Well look," said Keith, "there is a cell on my spur (part of the wing) this geezer can have, and that will put an end to this problem."

The screw said, "OK, Mr. Brooks," and after following us over agreed to notify the other guards that I was to be in this new cell.

Once the screw left the other inmate came back out of his cell with two cups of coffee. "Here brov," he said, "you look as if you've had a long day," handing me one of the cups, "my name is Keith Brooks."

As we were talking the other prisoners from the adjoining cells came out to meet me and introduce themselves, Keith's co-defendant Mark Wheeler, Gary Wilson, Alan King, also Jerry and Adam, these men were all in for drug-related offenses. And if I am honest with you, I never had a lot of time for non-Gypsies up until this point, but seeing the kindness and generosity these men showed me, accepting me into their circle, made me see things in a whole different light.

The next day I was assigned a job in the screen-printing shop, that was responsible for the manufacturing of all the signs used throughout the prison system, as Coldingly is a works prison having one of the largest industrial laundries in the UK, servicing most of the hospitals in and around London, also light fittings and various other activities. After a couple of weeks of this work, I was moved to the accounts section of the laundry that consisted of about an hour's work in the morning calculating the charges for the amounts of laundry that had been done.

Now between us we pretty much had the run of this prison. With Alan working in the kitchen, we were able to get one of the private workers straightened to bring our own food in, have it cooked in the kitchen and brought up to the wing for us to eat. Within days I had a mobile phone and small TV in my cell, and the screws, seeing we were clean and respectful people, would let us away with murder. For what you have to understand is these officers are used to dealing with the scum of the world in these places, so when sensible people or men who are in for money offences come along that just want to do their time as easy as possible and get out, they give them as much rope as they can. And with two visits a month, I was getting to see Lila and my girls on a regular basis. At this time my father and mother and most of my brothers and sisters were living and working in Europe, doing tarmac work in Holland and Germany, having been some of the first to enter East Germany when the Wall came down. This was a very prosperous time for my family, as this type of work was very much in demand in this part of the world at that time, spending the summers in northern Europe and moving further south in the winters, stopping off at places like Denmark and Norway in the north and Spain and France in the south, with my mother making her way home to see me in prison as much as she could, telling me how well they were all doing.

I think it was because I had listened to so many prison stories as a child from my father that this time I was to spend in prison seemed to be going easy, but it was to get a whole lot easier.

While weight training in the gym one evening with a couple of friends of mine – Yankee and Edwin, two black gangsters from north London who I used to play basketball with – we were approached by one of the gym screws asking if he could train with us. "No Gov, don't take this the wrong way but we can't be seen training with you," I said.

"Oh," he said, "sorry I didn't know that, it's just that I play rugby and I have a big game coming up, and could do with getting a bit fitter."

"I understand and in the normal world there would be no problem with you jumping in with us and lifting a few weights, but we are not in the normal world, and if we were to be seen associating with one of the screws other inmates might read something more into it; I hope you understand where I am coming from."

Now I had a couple of friends at this time from Coventry who played rugby for Warwickshire – Eric and George, who owned a ground works company that had done a lot of work for me on my site in Ryton-on-Dunsmore – and on mentioning their names to this screw, I noticed a strange look on his face. Asking me what my name was, he turned and walked away, thinking something I said must have upset him, then two minutes later he walked back over to me, saying, "Do you mind if I have a word in private?"

Wondering what his problem was, I said, "Yeah of course." Walking into his office he said, "I have someone on the phone who wants to speak with you." Handing me the phone I said, "Hello?"

"Hello Tony," said the voice on the other end of the line, "it's Eric."

Now it turns out that my mate Eric is this guy's best friend, telling me that he was best man at his wedding and godfather to his children and that he has told him I was a good guy and to offer me any help or assistance I may need. Before putting the phone down Eric said, "I hope to see you soon Tony and if I can do anything at all out here just let me know." Thanking him I put down the phone and said to the gym screw, "Well they say it's a small world don't they?"

CHAPTER THIRTY-SEVEN

After our chance meeting in the gym, this screw got me and my friends, Mark and Gary, the job in the gym, so once again I was the No. 1 Gym Orderly. Only in this gym I was to have my own office with television and phone, also a cooker that he had brought in for me, and he would meet Lila or one of her brothers each morning, and bring me in a bag of shopping, so as we were preparing and eating all our own food, with us having the likes of tiger prawns for starters, T-bone steaks for main course and a full cheesecake for dessert, all washed down with a bottle of my favorite red wine. As prison goes this was about as good as it gets, even getting me extra visits with Lila so as I had one each weekend. Time here seemed to be flying by with the months going by like weeks, but as you have heard me say before in this book, "All Good Things…" Oh, I am not even going to finish it.

Calling Lila one day she told me that she had been speaking to my sister Romain, and she was concerned that my brother-in-law Tommy was not doing his time so good and wanted to know if I could try and get to him. He by now had been moved to a semi-open C-category prison near Guildford in Surrey called Send. Telling her not to worry and that I would do my best to get to him, as I knew that after he had been sent to a lower category prison he would not be able to request a transfer back to a D-cat, so asking the screws to push through a transfer request for me. Within a week I was ready to go, with my good friends I had met in Coldingly begging me not to go. I set off for Send with the gym screw as one of my escorts. Stopping off at a pub restaurant on the way to have a drink and some food, he said, "Keep in touch, Tony, as I have really enjoyed your company. I just wish we had met under different circumstances."

Arriving at Send, they booked me in and escorted me round to the twelve-man dormitory where Tommy was located. Now this was a shock to me as I had only ever, apart from my first day in Winchester, been in a one-man cell. I now found myself sharing a dorm with eleven other men, and it was filthy, with the showers being so bad you would not go in them. Asking him what work he was doing, he told me he was working on an outside works party within the prison grounds, and that he had got me a place on his team. It was January and absolutely freezing outside. Telling me he was digging a trench for an electric supply, I laughed and said, "You would not pick up a shovel on a job when we worked together, and that was for a few quid; why the fuck would you dig a hole for £7.50 a week for this lot? Thanks but no thanks."

Looking round the dorm I said, "Which one of you is the dorm cleaner?" A young kid with long hair looked up and said, "I am. Why?"

"Well," I said, "you're sacked; the place stinks and if I am going to live here it can't be under these conditions, so you can take my place alongside Tommy on the outside works party and I will get this place up to scratch, OK?"

"OK," he replied.

For the next three days I scrubbed this dorm upside-down, having the screws bring me as much cleaning products as they could find, even pulling the fire hose from the hallway in to spray the walls of the showers, and asking them if I could use the dining hall floor polisher. By the time I was finished you could have eaten your dinner off the floor, never mind the tables, and once again the screws brought along one of the governors to see how clean it was. Again I was asked if I would like the job of being in charge of all the dorm cleaners. Declining their offer, I said, "No, Sir, I am happy with the job I have at the minute; besides, it's still not as clean as I would like it."

Getting my head down and doing my time, I made arrangements for Lila to move down from Coventry to Cranleigh, which was only about ten miles from the prison. Within a few months we were joined by Tommy's father Jimmy who had got time for similar offences and had himself moved to send to be with us, but within a few weeks was moved on because of being suspected of bringing alcohol into the prison hid in the roof of the prison tractor.

Winter turned to spring and after a visit from Lila I was told that an old friend of mine called Tommy Lee from Bagshot was trying to get to Send and had put a transfer request in. After hearing this I had a word with the screws to see if they could get him there. At this time having almost served half of my sentence I had applied to be put on work placement: this is a program where short-term prisoners are allowed to go and work for a local company, providing they pay a percentage of their wages to the prison, but before this you have to spend a few weeks doing a form of community service, doing work in the local area mostly for some type of charitable organization. I was allocated the job of doing up the local Red Cross facility, painting and decorating the hall both inside and out. Returning through the prison gates from work one day I was greeted by my old friend Tommy Lee who had arrived that day, having just spent the last few months in a closed prison. It was summer now and I was wearing shorts, a T-shirt and sunglasses. Having been working outside I was very suntanned: seeing me I will always remember his first words, "Well look at him, he looks like Elvis Presley," making us both laugh.

As time in prison goes this time spent together was quite funny at times, with us once again having the run of the place, with me being asked to sit on the prison board as the prisoners' representative, also being made the first super-enhanced prisoner in the history of Send. Like I said as long as you behaved yourself the guards would let you have your little perks, and turn a blind eye to a few bits and pieces. One of my funniest memories of my time inside was having Boxing Day with Tommy Lee, whose wife Janey had sent him in a new pair of pajamas/dressing gown and slippers, all blue and white pinstripes and I had smuggled him in the largest Cohiba Cuban cigar I could find as a Christmas gift, so dressed in his new outfit and smoking this giant cigar after a few drinks that one of the boys had brought in, we decided to take a walk over to the other wing to see some of our friends. Now you are not allowed to have anything in prison that you did not get from the canteen, so on reaching the door to the other wing, the screw on duty who had watched us walk across the yard, opened the door and said, "Hey Lee, who the fuck do you think you are, fucking Jimmy Cagney? Put that cigar out of sight before one of the governors sees it and I have to nick you."

Blowing a cloud of smoke into the screw's face as he walked by, Tommy said, "Don't be silly Gov, it's a canteen cigar." As we walked on we could hear the screw saying to himself, "They don't fucking sell Cuban cigars in the canteen."

It was during my time in this prison I was to have my first fight in prison. While playing five-a-side football in the gym one night, another prisoner called "Ratty" who had just been shipped there from Wandsworth prison in London, slide-tackled me, knocking me ten feet in the air, and landing on some benches that were stacked in the corner. This guy was a Jamaican Yardie, and for some reason wanted to get a name for himself within the prison as a hard man, so picking myself up I said, "Hey cunt, we're supposed to be having a friendly game of football here, not trying to cripple one another."

"Who you calling a cunt you Ras Clart?" – don't ask me what it means, I don't know, but that's what he called me.

"I am calling you a cunt," I replied. Now he started jumping up and down telling me what he was going to do to me, and none of it was good.

"Look," I said, "CUNT" – now really putting the emphasis on the word – "never mind shouting and screaming, let's me and you step into the recess (prison toilet) and have it out. The best man will walk out and the other will go to hospital."

Walking towards the recess door he now started shouting louder and louder until the gym screw on duty, who just happened to be a woman, came running into the gym, and seeing what was going on pressed the panic button on the wall. Within seconds nearly every screw in the prison came rushing in.

"What's going on?" said one of the screws.

"Nothing," I said, "just a silly little argument over a free kick is all," but this guy, now that the screws were there, really went into one, shouting what he was going to do, telling me, "You're dead you white bastard, honky motherfucker," and every other racist name he could lay his tongue to, now having to be dragged away by the screws, still shouting insults. I just stood there smiling, but deep down inside I was raging.

"Leave it Marshall," one of the screws said.

"What do you think I am, a fool, Gov?" I replied. "I am out of here soon. Do you think I am going to lose time over that piece of shit?"

The next morning I left the prison early as by now I had been granted work placement and was going to work every day, leaving at seven in the morning and returning at seven at night, after being given a job by a good old friend of mine, Nicky Smith from Chertsey. On returning that evening I was let in by one of the screws who I got along with very well, as some screws think they are would-be policemen and to others it is just a job of work.

"You had a row with Ratty in the gym last night Marshall, didn't you?"

"Yeah," I said.

“Well me and the other screws were talking about it, and you know if something was to happen to Ratty I don’t think anyone would give a shit. Between me and you he has been nothing but trouble since he has been here, and with his tough guy image I think he needs to be put in his place.”

Looking at him I said, “So if someone was to deal with Ratty would that someone get nicked?”

“No,” he said, “they would not, as I think all the officers on the wings this evening would be looking the other way, or distracted with other matters. In fact I bet if he was to have an accident no one would even see it.”

Nodding my head I walked into my dormitory, changed my clothes, putting on a track suit with hood and trainers, and then set off to find Ratty.

CHAPTER THIRTY-EIGHT

Walking out of my dorm, the officer turned his head away from me, and walking across the yard, any screws I came across did the same; reaching the door to the other wings it opened just as I got to it, with the screw once again turning his head as if not to see me. It was obvious that all the screws were in on it and could not wait to have someone deal with this guy that had by all accounts been bullying lots of other prisoners, and abusing everyone he came across. Walking from wing to wing it was like the doors were on remote control: without having to knock they opened just as I got to them. Reaching the wing where Ratty was on, I turned a corner and could see down the hallway was Ratty with his back to me waiting in a queue to use the phone, wearing a pair of headphones, with his head full of dreadlocks bouncing up and down in time to the music.

Moving as swiftly without running down the hallway as I could, I passed one of Ratty's friends who had been in the gym with him the night before, in seeing me he tried to warn Ratty, but he could not hear him because of the music. Just as I got to him as if by some sixth sense, he turned around, but it was too late: I hit him on the chin, dropping him to his knees, grabbed him by his dreadlocks and slammed his head into the wall, knocking him out cold. Pulling him by his hair I drug him into a small dormitory and jumped on his head, sending the headphone earpiece into his skull. Turning around I noticed that the occupants of this dorm were sitting at a table playing cards. One of them, it turns out, was a black friend of mine: looking at the other guys on the table with him he said, "Nothing to do with us, deal the cards."

Walking out into the hallway I made my way back to my dorm, with the same automatic doors as before. Leaving to go to work the next day I was met by the same screw that had let me in the night before.

"Alright, Marshall?" he said.

"Yeah I am fine, thanks," I replied.

"You won't believe it," he said, "but Ratty only went and had an accident last night."

"Really?" I said. "That's too bad."

"Yes they had to take him to an outside hospital," said the screw. "I don't think we will be seeing him again too soon. Anyway have a nice day," he said.

"Yeah I will," I replied, and off I went to work.

Within weeks half of the Gypsies doing prison in the south of England had either arrived or had put in transfers to come to Send, hearing that we had it good there, so our dormitory became like a hotel with only our friends allowed access. With two months to go in my sentence I was to make an error in judgment that would see me coming very close to spending a lot more time in prison.

Returning from work one evening at seven I walked in to find the two Tommy's and a few of the other Gypsy men having a drink, one of them being Albie Webb, the son of black Billy Webb, the man my father had fought with many years before. Albie was known to me from stopping on the site in Ryton-on-Dunsmore near Coventry some years earlier, and had made it quite clear that he had nothing to do with his father and family and did not want any trouble with me. In fact I saved his home from being beat up one day when some other Gypsy people came to have a fight with him, ending up with me seeing him fair play, and after winning his fight sent the people on their way. While sitting talking and drinking I got up to go to the toilet only to be followed in two minutes later by Tommy Frankham.

"You know that Albie's out there talking about your Dad, don't you?" he said.

"What?" I replied, "you're joking," thinking he was kidding.

"No I am not joking. He has just mentioned the fight his father had with yours years ago."

"He wouldn't do that," I said, "he has been in my company dozens of times and never said a word, why would he bring it up now?"

"Don't ask me," Tommy said, "but as your brother-in-law I had to come and tell you."

Walking out of the toilets thinking Tommy would not tell me lies, I confronted Albie: "What have you been saying about my father?"

"What?" he said with a look of total disbelief on his face, "Tony mush (man) I haven't said a word about your father."

Thinking if Tommy said he did, it must be right, I set into Albie, hitting him several times and knocking him out, onto the top of the pool table in the middle of the dorm. By now enraged with the thought that he would even speak my father's name, I walked back into the recess (toilet) and picked up a stainless steel bucket. Walking back in, I held the bucket in the air and brought it down as hard as I could onto Albie's head, losing count of the times I hit him in the head and body. If not for a good friend of mine running in and stopping me I think I may not have stopped until he was dead, saying, "That's enough Tony, you're going to kill him."

I threw the bucket down. Just as that the screw on duty came into the dorm. "What's going on in here?" he said.

"Albie's had an accident, Sir," said someone.

Picking him up, the screw carried him out of the dorm.

Waking up the next morning to go to work as usual, I reached the gate, only to be met by two screws who said, "No work for you today, Marshall: you're nicked for the assault of Webb."

Taking me straight to the block I couldn't help but feel like a total fool, as I only had three months left to do and I was out. After a couple of hours I was brought up in front of the Governor, Mr. Buchan, who as it turns out was from the same part of Scotland as my ancestors, and had been responsible for getting me the role of spokesman on the prison board.

"What's this all about Marshall?" he asked.

"I have nothing to say on the matter, Sir," came my reply.

"Well Marshall, two of my officers watched you assault another inmate, through the window of your dormitory last night, whose injuries are so bad we have had to take him to the Royal Surrey Hospital. Now I have to say I am quite astounded that this involves you, as you have been a model prisoner in your time here, and by the letter of the law I am supposed to call in the police and have you arrested and taken to an outside court for sentencing. But as I have said, you were up until this point a model prisoner, and in taking that into account I have made my mind up to be lenient on you. My guard who is at the hospital has said that Webb does not want to press charges, and I will have a word with the officers here who witnessed the assault, so as no further action will be taken. But I am duty bound to ship you back to the prison from which you came, until the end of your sentence."

Standing up he shook my hand: "Listen Marshall, off the record, as I have told my officers if you set about this man, there would have been a good reason for it, you're a sensible young man with your whole life ahead of you, too good to be in these places. Go to this other prison, get your head down, and get the fuck out, back to your wife and children, understand?"

Shaking his hand I said, "Thank you Mr. Buchan."

"Don't thank me, just do as I have asked, now on your way, and good luck," placing me back in the Block holding cell until such time as my things could be collected and transport arranged.

Hearing the voice of Tommy Lee, thinking he has come to ask to say goodbye, only for it to go quiet; then some time later I heard his voice again, shouting, "Is that you Tommy?"

"Yes," came the reply, "where are you?"

"Where am I? I am in the cell next to you."

"Why?" I asked.

"Because they are shipping me out with you."

Now it turns out that the screws had a suspicion that this fight was drink-related, and in putting two and two together had come up with Tommy's name as the source of supply, being as he worked on the outside prison party. Placing us in a minibus later that day, they shipped us both to Coldingly prison. On the way there I was telling Tommy, "Don't worry, everything will be fine, I know everyone in this prison and we can do as we like. It will be sweet as a nut."

By now it had been over a year since I had left Coldingly and in just that short period of time it had changed a lot, and for the worse I might add. After booking us in and speaking to one of the screws on my old wing I got us placed in two cells next door to each other. Walking into our cells, within two minutes my door came flying open and in stepped Tommy. "Never mind sweet as a nut, take a look out there" – pointing to the door – "it's like fucking Beirut."

Popping my head out the door I could see two inmates fighting in the hallway, with one grabbing the other and smashing his head through the window at the end of the spur. Closing the door I said, "Well they most certainly have let their standards slip, it seems they will let anyone in here nowadays," with us both laughing.

We sat down in my cell and played a game of cards. After apologizing to Tommy for him being shipped out along with me, we set our minds to what to do next. Meeting up with my old friend Gary who was still the Gym Orderly, we got him to get us anything we needed. Now the rules had changed since I was last here, and we now had to go through two weeks of induction classes, one each day, covering topics like health and safety, anger management and drug awareness amongst others. These classes were taken by people that did not want to be there as much as the prisoners, who were forced to attend, just turning up and going through the motions of instruction. So I devised a plan that if I was going to be made to do these classes I would make them work for their money, continually asking them to explain the points they were making over and over again, and then just when they thought it was over, saying, "You know what I still haven't got it, can you just run that by me one more time?" The best was having the health and safety teacher lift and re-lift a cardboard box over and over again in the correct way as to not damage your back: now come on we are grown men, I think we would know how to lift a box.

It was at one of these classes I was to meet one of the most feared and dangerous young men in the prison system at that time, known as Beefy. This young man, although only in his early twenties, had spent most of his life in one prison or another. For the crime of murder that he committed as a child, stabbing another boy when he was only thirteen, he was sentenced to "Her Majesty's Pleasure", which basically means he was serving a sentence of unknown quantity, until such time as the prison system feels he has learned his lesson. Sitting in the drug awareness class in which once again I was making the person who was taking it earn his corn, with question after question, then coming up with my own conclusion as to my thoughts on the matter, telling him that in my opinion drug addicts in prison should sue the prisons they are being held in for their condition.

"How do you come up with that?" said the course teacher.

"Well I will tell you how I have come up with this, Mr. Whatever-his-name-was, since the introduction of urine testing in prison for drugs use, you have turned an average prisoner serving a long sentence into a heroin addict."

Now with him and the rest of the class on the edge of their seats as to where this was going, I carried on. "People serving let's say a life sentence, recommended fifteen years; in order to get through this time will on occasion smoke a little puff to get them through such a long sentence, but because of the new urine testing system that can detect puff in your sample up to three weeks later, they are now switching to heroin that will only be there for two days, therefore cutting down on the chance of them getting caught and being sentenced to further time."

Seeing where I was going with this Beefy joined in with his view on the matter and said, "I am in total agreement with Mr. Marshall and think we should get a petition up with the thoughts of suing the prison system for putting us in harm's way from other drug-addicted inmates," which made us all laugh as Beefy was one of the most powerfully-built men I think I have ever come across, he was a clone for Mike Tyson, lisp and all; from the age of fifteen he had been the southern area powerlifting champion of Great Britain, going on to represent England in major powerlifting competitions.

Leaving the class Beefy looked at me and said, "You're a funny fucker and a clever cunt as well, you nearly had me going there for a minute."

For the rest of the week we continued to do the same thing, with me Tommy and Beefy bouncing off one another, making the classes more interesting. One night after a class while in my cell making a cup of coffee, without knocking in walked Beefy, who was renowned throughout the prison system as an enforcer/dept collector for the prison drug dealers. Closing the door behind him, with a strange look of anger on his face, he said, "Can I have a word Tony?" Now I did not know where this was going, but what I did know was that I had a monster of a man in my cell who looked angry, and I dint know with who.

"Yeah of course sit down Beefy," I said, "want a cup of coffee?" – thinking, "I wish this kettle would hurry up and boil, for if he is going to start on me the only option open to me is to throw it on him and run."

"Listen Tony," he said, "I would like to talk to you about something and I hope it will stay between us."

"Brother," I said, "I think you know me well enough by now to know I don't tell tales."

Nodding his head he started telling me of how he had got married in the last prison he was in, and of how he had just came off the phone to his wife, that they had argued over her wanting to go out with her friends in London, saying, "Well look Beefy she's a young woman and young women do go out. That's not to say she is going to do any harm, is it? And let's face it, you're in here, she could have went without telling you, and how would you have known? I think you need to be a bit more trusting."

Looking at me he said, “It is not just the going out that is the problem, you see she wants to go out and smoke crack with her friends.”

What I said: “Look Beefy, I think you’re talking to the wrong guy about this, I have never taken a drug in my life.”

“I know that Tony,” he said, “that is just the reason I came to you. Would you please do me a favour? Just speak to her on the phone for me and tell her what she is doing is not right.”

“OK Beefy, of course I will,” I said.

Walking down to the phones that were all being used, Beefy walked up to one of the men on the phone, and said, “Say goodbye.” Without a split-second delay the guy said to whoever was on the other end, “Goodbye,” and hung up.

Looking round to the queue for the phones that was about 30 long, he said, “You guys don’t mind if I jump back in, do you?”

“Oh no, no, no,” came the reply from everyone there, not daring to be the one to catch the brunt of Beefy’s bad mood.

Getting his girlfriend on the line he said, “I have someone here I want you to talk to, hang on,” handing the phone to me.

I said, “Look Beefy, I can’t talk to her with you stood over my shoulder; you go stand over there, and let me speak to her in private.” As he walked away I said, “Now listen, whatever your name is, this man is like a ticking time bomb, do you want him to get another life sentence and never come out?”

“No of course I don’t,” she said.

“Well then do as I say, if you want to go out and do whatever, you don’t have to tell him, because he is going to go off his head and hurt someone, so when I put him back on the phone you tell him you are going to behave yourself, you understand?”

“Yes,” she replied.

Calling Beefy back over I handed him the phone. After one minute of conversation he hung up. Walking over to me, he grabbed me and hugged me like a bear: “Thanks Tony, I knew I could count on you to sort that out for me. I owe you big time man,” he said.

Some time later Beefy was ghosted out of Coldingly (shipped out without warning), getting a message to me that he wanted to say goodbye. I made my way to the reception area just in time to catch him being loaded into the bus. Catching my eye he said to the guards escorting him, “Give me a minute.” One of them started to protest that they were running late, but after one of Beefy's looks, he changed his mind, saying, "Sure take your time Beefy."

Walking over with these guards in tow as they were double-cuffed to him, he reached out his hand: "You're one of the best guys I have met in all my time in prison," he said, "take care and keep in touch."

Shaking his hand I said, "You too Beefy, keep your head down and get yourself out of here."

"I will try," he said, and as that they loaded him into the van and drove away.

Some years later I was to learn that Beefy never did make it out of prison, finding him stabbed to death in his cell by multiple assailants. He was twenty-six years old.

CHAPTER THIRTY-NINE

With only eight weeks left of my sentence, I set my mind to getting as fit as I could. With Mark getting me a job in the gym, I decided to take part in training courses that were held in the gym, achieving top level awards in the teaching of weightlifting, and various other sports, passing the Pentathlete Award and Community Sports Leaders Award courses along the way, of which I still have the diplomas to this day.

Coming back to my cell one evening I stopped in to see how Tommy Lee was getting on. Entering his cell he introduced me to a man who had just moved into the cell next door to ours. Shaking hands with this man who Tommy said had come from Parkhurst prison on the Isle of Wight, he said, "I have just been telling Tommy I have a couple of pikey friends who live down the road from me at home. They're good old boys but you can't have a cup of tea off them because their homes are so dirty."

What I said – shocked by what I was hearing, as calling a Romany Gypsy man a "pikey" is like calling a black man a "nigger" – "Listen," I said, "mate, I don't know where you come from, but number one, don't ever call me a pikey again, and number two," I said, grabbing him by his arm and pulling him into my cell of which I had a dozen or so photographs of my home, wife and children on the wall, "that's my home and never mind take a cup of tea off me, you could eat your fucking dinner off my kitchen floor."

"Son," he said, "you have took me all the wrong way, I didn't mean no offence to you."

"No offence?" I said. "You have just insulted my whole race, because you know some stinky new-age Traveler who claims to be a Gypsy, you automatically tar us all with the same brush, now fuck off out of my cell."

About two hours later this same man came and knocked on my cell door, asking if he could have a word. Telling him to come in and have a seat, he said, "My son, I owe you a big apology, you are one hundred percent in the right, I was bang out of order saying what I did and I hope you can accept my apology and shake my hand and let us start again." He went on to say, "You see son, I like to think of myself as an intelligent person, and to think that I have insulted someone's race and creed, is as much a slight on me as it is them."

Looking at this man I could see how sincere he was in what he was saying, as some people will give you apologies and you can see they are just going through the motions, but not this man. I said, "You know in my opinion it takes a true man to admit when he is wrong and say sorry, and as far as I am concerned it is forgotten," shaking his hand.

He said, "My name is Joey Pyle."

Anyone who knows anything about London villains will know this man's name. Joey was serving eleven and a half years for conspiracy to supply Class A drugs, after being fitted up by one of his associates. After our initial disagreement we went on to become firm friends that lasted outside of our incarceration, with Joey going on to hold boxing events in the Kensington Garden Hotel in London, of which I and Lila were always guests of honor.

Joey was a true old-time gentlemen gangster, who would tell the story to anyone who came into our company of how in prison, while other people were smuggling in drugs, I was having fresh French stick bread, ham, cheese, olives and Black Forest gateau, with a good bottle of wine to wash it down, brought in for us. Sadly he was to pass away some years back, and is dearly missed.

After serving two years of my sentence I was to be released. One of the hardest things I had to do in prison was to say goodbye to my old friend Tommy Lee who had been shipped out with me from Send, telling him I hated leaving him behind. He said, "Don't be silly, I will be out soon enough, you get out there to your wife and kids and make up for lost time."

Finally the day arrived, and I walked out of prison a free man, with Lila there to pick me up. Heading to the car I stopped and turned around to have one last look at the place that had held me for so long and vowed never to go back. We traveled back to our home in Cranleigh in Surrey. On entering the lane to the site I could see yellow ribbons and balloons tied to every tree along the way, and on reaching home there was all my girls standing under a huge banner saying, "Welcome home Daddy". Stepping out of the car they all ran and jumped on me, cuddling and smothering me with kisses, all taking turns at saying to me, "Don't ever leave us again Dad."

"I won't," I said, "I promise."

After doing a few weeks of probation once a week, I was free to go and do as I liked, so after speaking to my father and brother Lee who were working in Norway at this time, I decided to take a trip over to see how I would get on working there. Catching a plane from London I made my way to Oslo, the capital of Norway, where my family were staying on a camping site that overlooked the whole of the city. After being locked up for two years I could not wait to get out there and make some money, so the next day bright and early I jumped in my brother Lee's jeep and went hawking, taking the first job I called into. Within a couple of weeks I decided to move over with my family, so returning home I bought a new Range Rover Jeep, Transit van and two new Talbert trailers, one for me and Lila and one as a bedroom for the girls. This was great times for not only were we all together as a family again, but I was going out getting a good living straight, as my brother was legal and registered to carry out work within Europe. After some weeks we decided to travel to Sweden. One of my fondest memories of this time was going across the fjord bridge that separates the two countries: it was like something you see on a postcard, with the log cabin houses dotted along the Scandinavian Peninsula.

With winter setting in, it was time to return to our home in the UK.

CHAPTER FORTY

Returning to Cranleigh, I made my mind up that I was not going to go back tarmacking, and after speaking with some friends who were making a good living bringing in imported cars from Europe, decided this was the job for me. Within a few weeks I had established a good network of suppliers and buyers.

Things were looking up and to top it all off Lila told me she was expecting again, which I was over the moon with, as what with being on bail for nearly three years and then spending nearly two years in prison, our twins were almost ten years old, so it was the right time to have another child, and to make it extra special after having tests we found out we were to have a son.

With my car trade going well, we settled into a way of life in Cranleigh, having our large home brought down from Coventry and being just across the road from my sister Romain and Tommy, who even after all our differences I still classed as my closest friend, treating him more like a brother than brother-in-law.

Summer turned to winter and along came Christmas time and with it came a phone call from my brother Lee, saying he had been out for a drink in Doncaster with all the men, and had got arguing with Billy Brazil (known as The Fox). Billy was the brother of Jim Brazil, my brother-in-law, who had been killed some years earlier in the car crash. After his death there had been some ill-feeling towards his treatment of his widow, Lila's sister Lucy. Apparently my name had been brought up in the conversation, and Billy had said something untoward that Lee had taken offence to. After telling me that there were too many to fight with, I said, "I will be there in two hours," jumping in my car. Tommy said, "I am coming with you," meeting on the way my brothers-in-law James and Joseph Doe and Tommy's brother Bobby.

We made it to Doncaster round about closing time of the pubs. Knowing that The Fox would still be in one of them having a late drink, we went from pub to pub in search of him, coming across him in a working man's club in the centre of town. Looking through the window I could see he was with several other Gypsy men known to me, one being Joe Boy Gaskin, a well-known young fighting man from the town. Laying out a plan that we would wait until he exited the pub then I would attack him, as the last thing we wanted was to be arrested for an affray in the public house.

Having another look through the window I was spotted by one of the other men. Knowing it was a matter of seconds before he forewarned The Fox and he might make an escape, I dashed into the pub and set to fighting with him, hitting him several times: he went down into a bench seat. As that the man who was drinking with him, Joe Gaskin, attempted to pull me off of him. Taking offence at this I drew back and hit this other person in the face, knocking him onto a table. As that the bouncers came running and grabbed hold of me, saying, "If you don't leave now we will have you arrested."

Walking out Joe Boy looked at me and said, "You shouldn't have hit me Tony."

"No," I said, "you shouldn't have got involved, but any way I did hit you so what do you want to do about it?"

Agreeing we would fight in the morning, I went back to my parent's house at Tilts Farm. Calling up first thing the next morning Joe Boy said, "If I come down will I get fair play?" And after giving him my assurance that he would, within half an hour he turned up.

Pulling our shirts off we stepped into the road of the site. Now I had not long come out of prison and was still very fit from all the training I had done inside, so moving around him and hitting him at will I felt this fight was going to be easy, but this man was well renowned as a fighter and was not going to go down without a fight. Getting over-confident I stepped in, thinking I would finish this quickly, and walked straight into a big right hand, that sent me sliding across the floor on my backside. Coming to a halt, Joe Boy's momentum carried him in my direction. Looking as though he was going to kick me, my brother-in-law jumped in front of him and pushed him in the face, telling him to get back. More shocked and embarrassed than anything else that I had been knocked over for the first time in my life, I rose to my feet, and said, "Come on, let's finish this fight."

Seeing this Joe Boy who I believe had just hit me with all he had, and I was still prepared to fight on, looked at me and said, "No I am not fighting any more, I don't think I am going to get fair play."

What I said: "Fight on, of course you're getting fair play." Shouting to everyone to stand back, I said, "Come on Joe Boy, that was a good shot but you will need more than that to win this fight."

Turning his back and walking away he said, "No, I am not fighting any more, I will give you best." Walking after him I said, "No fucking way are you knocking me down and giving me best, fight on."

"No," he said, reaching his car.

I said, "OK, if you don't think you're going to get fair play we will drive off in your car and finish the fight wherever you feel comfortable."

Getting into his car that his wife was in along with his cousin John Cunningham who had come to see him fair play, I said, "Drive – we will leave everyone else here and finish the fight on our own."

Again he said, "No I have told you I have give best and that's it, I don't want to fight you again."

Looking at him I said, "If you don't finish this fight now I will come back and next time there will be no fair play, I will give it to you with whatever I can lay my hands on, understand?"

"Well we will have to cross that bridge when we come to it Tony, now please let me go."

Stepping out of the car, he sped away as fast as he could. Returning home that day I could not get it out of my head that I had been knocked down by this man, my pride was dented and I had to do something about it, with my mother-in-law saying to me, "If you don't fight now, you will have to have many fights."

As if having a sixth sense of what was to come, jumping in my car that following weekend, I traveled up to Doncaster on my own. Driving to the site at Thorne where Joe Boy lived I knocked on his door, with his wife answering. I asked, "Is Joe Boy in?"

"No," she replied, "he is out."

"Bit early to be out," I said, "isn't it?"

"He has gone coursing (hunting with dogs) and left first thing this morning."

"Give me his mobile number," I asked.

"He don't have it on him, he has left it here," she said.

Not wanting to row with a woman, I said, "Well when he comes back tell him I am here to fight him again. Tell him I am on my own, and will come and meet him anywhere he wants, tell him I will stay in Doncaster until I hear from him, I don't care how long it takes."

"OK," she said, "I will tell him."

Giving her my mobile number for him to call I drove away. Phoning a few of the boys in Doncaster to find out where he was coursing with no luck, I did a round of the pubs, finally turning up at an Irish Traveler's house in Doncaster by the name of Willy McGinley who was a friend of Joe Boy's, asking him if he would do me a favor and give Joe Boy a call, and get him to come and have a fight with me. "Tony I don't really want to be involved but as you have asked me I won't refuse you."

Calling Joe Boy he said, "Look this man is here on his own, and wants to fight you, come down to mine and me and the boys will see you fair play; you can fight in my yard."

With Joe Boy asking to speak to me, Willy handed me the phone. "Look Tony, why are you doing this? I have told you I don't want to fight you again," he said, "I have left Doncaster, so don't bother looking for me anymore."

Telling him, "If you don't come and fight me now, I have told you what will happen, haven't I?"

"Yep," he said, "and I have told you, we will cross that bridge as and when."

Putting the phone down, I got in my car and drove home. Some years later me and Joe Boy did meet again, and as I had forewarned the outcome was not too good – *for him*.

With Lila booked into the Princess Margaret Hospital in Windsor, finally the day arrived: my son Antony Santino Joseph James was born on the 23rd January 1998. Being there for the birth as I had been for all of my children, I felt as if I was the luckiest man alive to finally have the son and namesake I had so longed for, and what a son he was: weighing in at nearly nine pounds, he looked like a little bear, with olive-colored skin, and the most perfect features, having what looked like a crew-cut hairstyle. Taking him from the nurse I gazed into his eyes and once again my heart melted as it had done with all of my children, for I believe there is no love in the world as the love you feel for your children, these small people who you have brought into this world, so dependent on you for everything, and so full of love for you. In my opinion a love that has no measure and cannot be replaced.

Leaving Lila in hospital with the baby I drove the girls and my mother-in-law Zenda back home, then headed to the pub to wet the baby's head, with nearly everyone who knew me traveling far and wide to come have a drink with me to celebrate the birth of my first son. After the pub closing time, me, my brother Lee and his wife Michele, sister Romain and Tommy, brother-in-law Joe Doe, and

Tommy's brother Sam Frankham and his wife, went back to the hotel my brother was staying at in Guildford, to carry on drinking, as I said, I was overjoyed at the fact Lila had given me a son, and felt over the moon, and relaxed in the company I was in. This as it was to turn out was a big mistake.

With Romain and Michele going up to the room to talk, us men carried on drinking in the bar. After some time Tommy and Joe got up to go to the toilet, returning some time later, but instead of rejoining us at the table they stopped up at the bar. Looking over I could see a strange look on Joe's face, with Tommy now looking as though he was arguing with him.

"What's wrong?" I asked.

"Oh nothing," replied Joe, "we are just talking," with Tommy now looking more and more aggressive.

I said, "Come and sit back down, what's the matter Tommy?"

Looking at me he said, "Nothing's the matter with me."

"Well come and sit back down, let's not spoil a nice night."

"We will sit down in a minute," he said, "I am just telling Joe something."

Now paying more attention to what was being said I caught the words, "smashed my trailer up", obviously referring to his trailer being smashed up at Goodwood, some years earlier. Now standing up I said to Joe, "Come away Joe, come sit down." With Joe now joining us at the table I looked back over to Tommy and said, "Come and sit back down, forget about all this silliness tonight."

"I don't want to sit down," he said, so standing up and walking over to where he was stood I said, "Well then I will stand up too. What's wrong? Why are you bringing all this old shit up tonight? My boy has just been born and we are supposed to be having a good time."

One word followed another and before you know it we were fighting again. Now I have never declared myself to be a fighting man, but the Tommies of this world are no good to me. After hitting him a few times I caught a glimpse out of the corner of my eye of his brother Sam coming towards me with a vodka bottle in his hand. Not able to move out of the way in time, he smashed it into my head and the lights went out.

I awoke to find myself in the Royal Surrey Hospital, with a surgeon working on me. It turns out the bottle had broken and cut me very badly, with cuts through my eyelid, nose, lip, and a seven-inch open wound down my neck. Asking me to keep as still as possible as the cut on my neck had only just missed my jugular vein, the doctor worked for some hours stitching me back together. Taking me into a recovery room I was met by my mother-in-law, who informed me that all the boys were locked up and that a police officer was waiting to question me. Looking over I could see Tommy's brother Young Fat Jimmy Frankham was there too. Calling him over I said, "Look what they have done too me, the fucking cowards, but never mind that I will deal with them later."

Asking my mother-in-law to go get the policeman, and telling Fat Jimmy to stay so as he could hear what was being said, I asked the policeman, "Why have you got my family locked up?"

"Well we believe, from the evidence and statements taken from the hotel staff, that you have been the victim of a major assault this evening."

Asking him if he had his notepad handy, as I wanted to make a statement. My statement was this: "Me and my brother and brothers-in-law were horsing around play-fighting, I lost my footing and fell through a glass table with bottles and glasses on it, cutting myself in the process. Understand, that is my statement, so I suggest you go release my family members immediately. Now fuck off."

Looking at Young Fat Jimmy I said, "And you can fuck off with him, there ain't no grass lying in this bed." Signing myself out of the hospital that night, against the doctor's wishes as I had severe concussion, my mother-in-law drove me home.

One of the hardest things I have ever had to do was see the look of horror on Lila's face the next day on going in to her hospital to see her and the baby, telling her what had happened. Crying, she said, "My boy has just been born and you could have died," and looking in the mirror I looked like Frankenstein's Monster, with over 30 stitches in my face, neck and head. But the thing that caught my eye more than any of the injuries was a print mark on my cheek of the sole of a Timberland boot, for this meant that even when I was knocked out by the bottle, Tommy still had stamped on my face. How do I know it was Tommy, you may ask? Because the Timberland boots he was wearing me and Lila had bought him for his Christmas present only one month before.

Later that same day Tommy and Sam's father and mother Big Jimmy and Hazel Frankham came to see me at Lila's hospital, with Jimmy having a look of disgust on his face at what his sons had done, for although some people may beg to differ, me and Jimmy were good friends, having spent a lot of time in each other's company what with working together and prison. Speaking to Jimmy he said, "This shouldn't have happened Tony but it has, what do you want to do about it?"

"Look Jimmy," I said, "it was only a drunken fight and if Sam had not hit me with a bottle, we probably would all be talking this morning, but the fact is he did, and could have killed me the day my son was born, and that I can't forgive, Jimmy. Now in my opinion the only way this can be put right is for you to bring Sam along to me, I will smack him in the mouth and that will be the end of it."

Jimmy said, "If you promise you won't hit him with nothing or cut him, that will do," shaking my hand.

At that moment Lila's Aunt Hazel looked up and said, "No, you won't smack my boy in the mouth, you can fight any of the other boy's but not him."

"None of the other boys hit me with a bottle," I replied, "but if they did I assure you it would be them I would be fighting, and besides I am not talking about fighting Sam when you bring him to me I probably won't waste my time hitting him, but he has to be held accountful for his actions, no one else, and if you don't finish it this way, when I do bump into him then I will not be accountful for my actions."

Now Jimmy knew this was a good deal, and was keen to accept it but was overruled by Hazel, once again saying, "No you are not hitting my baby," even though he was 26 at the time.

"OK then, Tommy can take his place," I said. "Give me a few days to let my cuts heal and have the stitches removed, then we will deal with it."

"OK," said Jimmy, "I would rather you didn't fight and if there was any way I could turn back the clock, so as this didn't happen I would, and if there is any way we could just forget about it and put it behind us."

"Jimmy," I said, "look at the state of me, can you see the boot mark on my face?"

Nodding he said, "Yes."

"You know what that means don't you?" Once again he nodded. "Could you forget it?" I asked.

"No," he said. Standing up, he shook my hand and said, "Goodbye and give me a call when you're ready."

Within a few days Lila and Tony Jr were released from hospital. Taking them home I felt unwell, as since the hit on the head I had been suffering from bouts of dizziness as I was still quite badly concussed. Two days after bringing Lila and the baby home, I could not contain my anger anymore, with the events of that night playing over and over in my mind, with the thoughts of how this man that I had put so much love and friendship into could do this to me, and instead of coming to me and begging forgiveness, and saying sorry, it seemed as though he was enjoying the moment in the limelight. Trying to put this into perspective in my head, I was approached by a very good friend of Tommy's who had phoned me up to say he had been asked by Tommy to come along to fight with me, and that the Frankhams were rounding up as many people as they could muster to come along, but that he had refused to be involved, and had asked, "Is Tony bringing a gang?" Being told no, he then said, "So why are you taking a gang to him?"

"Listen," he said, "I am just marking your card, he ain't coming on his own."

Thanking him I said, "I can't believe what they are doing."

"Tony," he said, "you have beat Tommy twice, and let's face it you were not losing the other night or why would Sam hit you with the bottle? Now put the shoe on the other foot, if Tommy had beaten you, wouldn't you want revenge?"

This only threw petrol on my already burning desire for retaliation, thinking all this time I was treating him like a brother, he was scheming behind my back, just waiting for a weak moment or an opportunity to have his payback. So later that evening phoning to big Jimmy's where Tommy had been hiding out since the fight, I said, "Bring him through tomorrow morning, I want this over and done with."

Tommy, taking the phone from his father, said, "Oh I will be through tomorrow alright, I have waited a long time for this."

"Well from what I have just been told, I would believe that," I said, "I have also been told you're bringing a gang with you to my home with my new-born baby inside."

"Well as I see it the more the merrier," was his reply.

"OK," I said, "bring who you want, they can't fight your fight for you, I will be here on my own waiting, no problem."

Within minutes of the fight being on for the next morning my phone never stopped ringing, from friends and family asking to come along to support me. I replied, "No," thanking them for their kind offer, but telling them I don't want no one else involved, knowing that all Tommy wanted to do was deflect the fight away from him, and make it into a gang fight, and no way was I going to let that happen, with Lila having murders with me, saying, "How can you fight? You have concussion and haven't slept all week."

I said, "Look, I have to do this."

One of Lila's aunts phoned and said, "Does he know they are bringing an army of men to his door?"

"Yes," Lila said, "and my baby is in this home."

"Call the gavvers (police)," Lila's aunt said, "get them locked up coming to you like that."

Lila replied, "He won't do that, you know what he is like about the gavvers."

That evening Lila's father John Doe and two sons, my brothers-in-law James and Joseph turned up, to be with us, and first thing the next morning as I waited outside my home, up pulled my father and mother who by now were in their seventies – telling them, "You should not have come," only to be told, "You're our son, where do you think we are going to be?"

Ten minutes later up pulled my brother Lee and sister Nicky, and my cousins from Tiptree Marky and Jimmy and Nelson Taylor who were equally as close to Tommy as they were to me, telling me, "We have only come to watch fair play for the both of you."

With the fight supposed to be on for seven in the morning, that time came and went. Getting a call from Tommy's friend, who had phoned me earlier, he told me, "They are at the train station in Guildford waiting on all their people turning up, oh and by the way they are heavily armed."

CHAPTER FORTY-ONE

At ten o'clock up pulled a car with Young Fat Jimmy Frankham, John Frankham, and Lila's cousin Toucher Doe, who was my father-in-law's brother's boy. Getting out of the car, Fat Jimmy said, "Right we are here, do you want a fight or a war?"

Laughing at him I said, "Who are you going to have a war with? You could hardly get out of the car you fat cunt."

As that Lila's cousins from Newark in Nottinghamshire, Joe Boy, Roy Boy, Ivan, France and Harry Botton drove up. Getting out of the car they looked at me and said, "We have not come here to fight against you Tony, Lila is our cousin as much as Tommy and we would rather see you not fight and try and stop it."

Explaining to them that as I saw it, this was the only way to put an end to it by having a square go with Tommy, and putting it behind me, saying once again, "Look at me, would you forgive it? I don't know why he has brought all these people, look who I have, and even them I told not to come."

Looking at me Ivan said, "Well never mind who you have with you, I will see you fair play, because I make you right, talk again or not talk again, have a fair fight here today and that's the end of it."

Shaking his hand I said, "That will do me, let's go."

Walking down the site at Cranleigh, I could not believe how many people they had brought along with them, hundreds, but I did not care one bit: all I wanted was to have my fight fair and square, and then I could put it out of my mind and get on with my life. Reaching an empty plot of land, with the men forming a ring, me and Tommy stepped inside.

Looking around at this crowd of men who were all baying for my blood, then looking back at Tommy I smiled at him, thinking, "You thought because you bring all these men with you, it might make this go away, but here we are just you and me."

Starting to fight I knew I had to fight a much different type of fight than I had ever fought before, as every time I hit him with a good shot, the reaction of the crowd was as if they could rip me apart. So thinking to myself, "If I knock him out there is a good chance that this gang will not only beat me to death but the people who are with me as well, my father, mother, father-in-law, brother-in-laws, brother and sister, cousins and friends who would not run and leave me, no matter what" – not to mention Lila, who was never more than ten feet away from me throughout the fight – so I resigned myself to the fact I would just wear him down and make him give me best, and that in front of all his supporters who came for him, he would have to walk away a beaten man.

Now bear in mind that Tommy was a very skilled boxer who during his career had hundreds of amateur bouts, and went on to box several times as a pro, so my task was no easy one, but I knew that I was the fitter of the two, because of all the training I had done to fight Joe Boy Gaskin some weeks before. So standing my ground and letting Tommy tire himself out dancing around, it was not too long before he started to lag. Seeing this I stepped up the pace slightly, and made him work that little bit more. Remember I had concussion and every shot he did land with felt like I had been hit with a sledgehammer, but I was determined I was not going to lose.

Now tiring even more, Tommy grabbed hold of me, but fighting inside he was no match for me, so after landing a couple of good shots, his cousin jumped in and pulled us apart, and hit me several times with his elbow in my eye, busting open the stitches in my eyebrow. Enraged by this all thoughts of winning the fight by making him give best went out the window: stepping into Tommy, I hit him with a flurry of punches that sent him back into the crowd. Seeing this, Johnny Frankham who was supposed to be watching us fair play, jumped in between us, pushing me back.

"Hold it," he said, "stop fighting here and come around to the field next door and finish the fight."

Now this is the oldest trick in the book, allowing Tommy the chance to get his second wind.

"What?" I said, "we have been fighting here for 25 minutes, why would we go around to the field? Fight on," I said to Tommy.

Stepping around Johnny Frankham, I flew back into Tommy, hitting him with good shots. The crowd, sensing he was now on his last legs, ran into me, grabbing and pulling at my arms, holding me back and allowing Tommy free shots at me, with Ivan doing his best to keep them off of me, but being pulled about himself. The crowd was on the verge of losing control. Seeing this, my father pulled a handgun from under his coat and shot it into the air, shouting, "Get your fucking hands off of my boy."

Hearing the gun go off, 99% of this bunch of bullies that had come along ran like rabbits, knocking down fences as they tried to get away.

"Anyone else puts their hands on my son I will blow their fucking heads off," my father said.

One man and one man alone walked forward, Big Jimmy Frankham. "There is no need for guns, Johnny," he said to my father.

"No need for guns? My boy is supposed to be getting fair play here today, is that what you call fair play? Come on," my father said to me, "this fight's over, you can fight another time on your terms."

Walking back to my home some minutes later up the road came Tommy with a relative of his that was known as a gunman. On reaching us I said to my father, "See him, he will have a gun on him."

Pointing his gun at the man, my father said, "Who him? If he even looks like he is going for a gun I will blow him in two."

Seeing the gun being pointed at him this man said, "Whoa, I haven't come for none of this; Tommy just wants to speak to you."

"OK," I said, "speak."

"I want to come home to my place," said Tommy, "can we shake hands and forget about this?"

"No," I said, "we can't."

"Please, for the sake of the kids, let's forget about it," he asked.

Walking over to Lila, I said, "What do you think?"

Looking at me, she said, "He is married to your sister, his kids are like our own, let it go, you don't have to be friends, but for the sake of your sister, let it go."

Shaking his hand, I said, "You will never be in my company again, but as far as I am concerned it is over."

Turning around, he walked back down the road to where the rest of his gang were waiting. They all got in their cars and left, waiting a couple of weeks at his parents' before returning home.

One evening late at night, waiting until my sister had put the kids to bed, I ran up into his home. Finding him sitting in a chair in his front room, I pulled a gun from my waistband. Putting it to his forehead, I said, "Look at me, by all rights I should blow your fucking head off for what you have done to me, but for the sake of leaving my sister a widow and my nephew and nieces without a dad,

I am going to let you live, but don't ever look in my direction again, or it might be a different story understand?"

"Yes," he said.

Turning I walked out, never to speak to him again. Now some people reading this may be thinking why I have never sought any act or form of retribution against these men. The fact is I made a promise to someone, that as long as they are alive I will not seek revenge; but in the words of my late brother-in-law Jim Brazil, "It is a long road that does not have a turn." And I am a very patient man.

Sometime after this trouble Big Jimmy Frankham was to die of a massive heart attack. Lila phoned and asked if I could come and pay my last respects to him and attend his funeral. I was refused, but no matter what went on with me and his sons, Jimmy was and always will be held in the highest regards and respect by me, as an old friend.

CHAPTER FORTY-TWO

Returning from spending the following Christmas and New Year in Disney World Florida, whilst driving back to our home in Surrey, Lila looked at me and said, "You know what, normally after a long holiday I am looking forward to going home, but after all the trouble with Tommy (to whom I was still not speaking) I am not looking forward to it at all."

Pulling off the road and stopping I said, "Is that how you really feel Lila?"

"Yes," she said.

"Well if that's the case you won't ever have to spend another day there."

Taking her and the kids to the nearest hotel, I got back in the car and drove over to an old friend of ours called Joe Mitchell, who had a campsite in Essex that me and Lila had visited, and both been taken with. Doing a deal with him to exchange the camp for my place in Surrey, we shook hands, and within a couple of days we moved in.

It was about this time I took in a partner by the name of Percy Smith, as the car trade was doing well and I needed someone to help with the sales. Percy was someone who I had known for some years, and seemed a nice, kind and genuine person. With business going from strength to strength we became firm friends, taking family holidays together and attending his sons' weddings, even taking him along to watch my football team Manchester United win the treble in 1999, of which the Champions League final was held in the Nou Camp in Barcelona. Booking into a hotel just outside of Barcelona in a seaside town called Sitges, we found that the whole of the Man U team where staying in the same hotel for three days before the match. This was like a dream come true for me and my brother in law Joe, as we are lifetime Man U fans, so spending the days talking to them around the pool was fantastic. Coming back from a meal one evening, we walked into the bar to find Roy Keane, who was the captain of United at that time, sitting drinking with Henning Berg another top player and their head of security at that time, called Ned Kelly.

Walking over to Roy I shook his hand and asked him, "Roy do you mind if I ask you a question, are you a Traveler?" As there had been plenty of rumors that he was.

"No," he said, "I am not, but I wish I was, as I have many Traveler friends, both in Ireland and in Manchester."

Inviting us to sit down, we talked for hours. With him being suspended for the final he was putting away the pints of lager for fun.

At the end of the evening I said, "Roy I would buy you another pint but the bar's closed."

He looked at me and said, "Never mind that." Leaning forward he pulled out from under his seat a full crate of beers. Handing me and the boys one each, he said, "Get that down your necks."

I have to say he was one of the nicest guys you would ever care to meet, and a true gentleman in front of the women, not even swearing in front of Lila or the other women that were there.

Another memory that will last with me forever is sitting talking by the poolside with David Beckham for hours, with him being equally as big of a gentleman as Roy, getting up to buy us drinks, and having pictures taken. While sitting with him people would keep coming asking for his autograph or to have a photo taken with him. He never refused once. Saying to him, "That must drive you mad sometimes David," I will never forget his reply. "Tony," he said, "some of them people have probably drove miles to see me, who am I to refuse them? Let's face it, I am not royalty, I kick a piece of leather around a field for a living."

I said, "Yeah but you can't half kick that piece of leather David," making us all laugh. He was another true gentleman, and a credit to our nation.

Winning the treble that year is one of my greatest sporting memories: being there to watch it unfold, with us winning in the dying seconds, will stay with me forever.

Returning to England and after taking my brothers-in-law James and Joseph into the business with me, things were going along fine. Having fully settled into our new life in Essex, developing the site further and having a new large twin unit delivered, it felt like home. By now my eldest daughter Lila Tawny was sixteen and had started attending the fairs and dances with all the other kids, and with Lila's mum and dad and brothers and their families coming to live with us, and me and Lila buying her sister Lucy a new trailer and car, we had her moved onto the site with us also, with the girls having my girls for company and young Jim making friends with the other young Gypsy men on the site, life was good for us all.

On turning sixteen I bought my nephew Jim Brazil a new transit van for his birthday, we were all together as one big family, and with my father and mother having bought and settled down on a piece of land in Bawtry near Doncaster, but pulling on my place quite often, as my father had suffered a few minor strokes over the last few years, and on occasion my mother needed a little break away from Doncaster, things could not be much better.

It was around this time that my nephew Jim Brazil started getting into trouble, having fights with other Gypsy boys. It seemed as though he was having a fight nearly every weekend of his life, with me and his uncles running from one end of the country to the next to see him fair play, even on occasion going with him to fight with the sons of old friends of mine, asking him, "Son, I have known these people a very long time, why are you falling out with them?" with him saying that the boy had been cheeky and he had to fight. And as the saying goes, "Blood is thicker than water": me and his uncles would be there by his side, giving him our full support, and with me and his uncles' reputations as being men to be reckoned with, he had one of the best support systems within the Gypsy fighting community, a system that in my opinion he used and abused at times, for turning up to some of these fights his opponent was beaten before even putting his hands up, for fear of what the recourse would be for winning against him.

It was at one of these fights, I was to meet up with my old adversary Joe Boy Gaskin. Turning up to watch a fight between Henry Francis and one of the Beaches in Doncaster one day, the fight was changed around to Jim fighting a young man by the name of Abraham Vary, and whilst waiting for Abraham and his followers to turn up, I was to learn that Joe Boy had been fighting with his cousin John Cunningham, who as you may recall was the person who came to see him fair play against me, and was on the phone to John saying he was going to come along and that John had him to fight today as well. Taking the phone from John Cunningham, I said, "Hello Joe Boy, never mind coming down to fight John, I am here waiting to fight you, so get yourself over here and let's take care of our unfinished business. There are hundreds of people here to see you fair play this time, so you can't have any more excuses."

Saying once again, "I don't want to fight you," he put the phone down.

After waiting some time for Jim's opponent to travel to Doncaster for the fight, finally he arrived with about one hundred followers. Using an empty plot of land with a wall around it as the arena, the fight was on. After fighting for a few minutes the crowd surged forward, and in trying to get them to stand back, we noticed that a few of the members of their gang had weapons, with one in particular drawing a large knife from his coat. Seeing this all thoughts of fair play went out the window, with a member of our gang pulling a gun and, hitting this knife carrier over the head with it, the gun went off.

Once again as in the past, when a gun is fired most of the crowd disperses, running for cover. As the crowd evaporated parting like the Red Sea, lo and behold who was standing right in front of me, none other than Joe Boy? Give him his dues, he had pulled off one of the cleverest moves I had ever seen at a fight, for as everyone's attention had been on Jim's fight, he had drove up, pulled John Cunningham away from watching the fight, and was now in the process of beating him to within an inch of his life. Running towards him, he saw me coming and turned to face me. Both throwing shots at the same time, but with mine connecting, he dropped to the floor; standing over him I said, "I told you to come out and fight me and you would get fair play, and I also told you what would happen if you did not."

As that I withdrew from my pocket a lead truncheon, and proceeded to beat him with it, only stopping when his father Bob who had been a well-known fighting man in his day stepped forward, grabbing me by the arm, and said, "Tony he has had enough, you're going to kill him, please stop."

"OK," I said, "take him away Bob."

Getting in our cars we traveled home to Essex and for the time being some peace and quiet. With Lila Tawny meeting and getting engaged to a young man by the name of James Russell from Winchester, it was decided we would have the wedding at home, in our back paddock. Having a huge marquee set up and after inviting over four hundred people to attend, she was to be married in Waltham Abbey on the 6th of August 2004 with her sister Montana as bridesmaid, and the rest of her sisters and cousins being maids of honor.

The day arrived: seeing her in her wedding dress, she looked like a beautiful princess, as I am sure anyone who has ever gave their daughter away to be married will attest, it is a feeling of huge happiness that she has met someone she loves and wants to spend the rest of her life with, mixed with the feelings of deep sadness that you are giving away in a sense one of your most prized possessions. The day went off without a hitch, with all of our most treasured friends and family in attendance, with everyone who came saying it was the best wedding they had ever been to. After the wedding, while Lila Tawny was on honeymoon, me and Lila went on a holiday to get over the wedding and some weeks after returning, she gave me the wonderful news that she was expecting again and we were going to have another baby.

While speaking with my brother-in-law James one day he was to tell me about a person he had come across, who he would like me to meet. This man was in the telecoms business in a major way, but had developed a drug abuse problem and got himself in some form of trouble with the local dealer, and had asked James if he could sort it out for him. Bringing this man to meet with me, it soon became apparent that this person was a super-brain that had gone off the rails. Sorting out his problem for him, he asked, "How much do I owe you?"

"Nothing," I replied, "but what I want is for us to make some money together, with the use of your knowledge and experience, and our funding."

Agreeing to this we set up a plan of action: bringing along some friends of mine who were trained telecoms engineers to meet with this man, he told us of how he was the inventor of a system called Gate Way Minutes. Without boring you with the intricate technical ins and outs, and in trying to put it in layman's terms, these were machines that you loaded with contract mobile SIM cards, of which you had a bundle of international minutes; these machines could be connected up to landlines, therefore transferring the call for use on the mobile minutes.

I know, when I first heard this it went straight over my head too, but the top and the bottom of this was that you could sell these minutes for huge profits, so with our engineers on board we set up a company and started supplying some of the top companies in London. Within weeks this work took off in a major way, until at one point we were the third largest supplier of airtime minutes in the

UK, with only Tesco and Sainsbury's being in front of us. Setting up an office in Harlow with a direct link to a telecoms hub in London, things were going fantastic. Putting myself on the books of this company with a wage of several thousand pounds a week after tax, business could not have been better, and to top it all off Lila had given birth to my second son "Santino Joseph Marshall", born on the 11th May 2005, in The Portland Hospital in London. This was the cherry on the cake as far as I was concerned: with my beautiful girls all grown up and our two wonderful sons, our family was now complete, and as I have said business was going along great, but in my private life things were about to take a major turn for the worse.

Lila's father John had been suffering for some weeks with as he would describe it, a bad back, in actual fact the problem was ingrown hair follicles in the base of his back which is a most common ailment of dark-haired men. For several years he had had this problem that would flare up every now and again, but after taking a course of antibiotics it would go away. Me and James would pull up to speak to Uncle John ("Uncle" being the term that all younger Gypsy people are taught to call their elders) one day asking him how he felt. He said, "Not too well, Tony. If it doesn't get any better by this evening I am going to go to the hospital."

"Never mind waiting till this evening," I said, "jump in now and me and James will take you and wait with you till you're seen."

"No, no," he said, "you have things to do, and besides it will probably be better later on."

Leaving to go to work, we would get a call from Lila that afternoon to say that her dad had been taken to the hospital and they were keeping him in. Leaving what we were doing and traveling straight to the hospital, we went in to see Uncle John, with James saying, "He must be bad because you know how much he hates hospitals, don't you?"

Finding John in a wing we spoke to the doctor who was dealing with him, being told that it was only that the in-growing hair follicle had gotten infected, that they would be putting him on an antibiotic drip to clear it up, and that they would be keeping him in overnight. After spending a couple of hours with him and with the nurses starting to get upset, Uncle John said, "You lot go home now and come back to pick me up in the morning."

Saying goodbye none of us could have predicted what was to happen next. Having only just arrived home from the hospital my phone rang. It was the doctor who was attending to Uncle John, who informed me that they had a specialist take a look at my father-in-law and it seems the problem was far greater than he had diagnosed, and that they had rushed him down to theater for an emergency operation. Shocked and dumbfounded at this turn of events, we all rushed back to the hospital.

Some hours later the surgeon who was working on Uncle John came out to talk to us, telling us that the ingrowing hair follicle had become badly infected and turned to septicaemia – poisoning John's blood system – and that they were fighting to save his life. Now this was too surreal, as when we had left him only 20 minutes earlier he had been sitting up in bed talking to us, and to think he was now fighting for his life was beyond comprehension. After hours spent removing the damaged tissue from around the base of his back the doctor came back out to tell us they had saved his life, but that he was still gravely ill, and would require several more operations in the coming days to get the infection under control. Moving him onto the critical wing, we were allowed to visit him, telling him what had happened. He seemed in as big of a state of shock as we all were, but with the doctors assuring us that they were doing all they could, and with what looked as though he might make a full recovery, we felt that with a bit of luck he would pull through.

Day after day went by with the whole family never leaving his side. Then one day after taking a turn for the worse and being moved onto the high-dependency unit, the doctors came to speak to us, telling us that his condition was now critical and even though they were doing all they could, we had to prepare for the worst. Looking at the doctors I said, "Please do your very best to save him; he is the head of our family and is a good man who is truly loved by us all."

With Uncle John now slipping away, the doctors came and told us to say our goodbyes. After everyone had kissed and hugged him for the last time, I took his hand, holding it tight. I whispered in his ear, "Don't you worry about nothing my uncle John, I will look after everyone, you go now and I will see you soon, I loved you like a father and I will never forget you."

Some minutes later he was gone, with all of his family around him. He lost his bravest of the brave fight for life, leaving a hole in all of our lives that will never be filled, but leaving us with some of the greatest and funniest of memories that will stay in our hearts forever.

After the sudden death of Uncle John, it was as if someone had pulled the rug out from underneath all of us, with Lila being inconsolable. What with the baby just being born and the loss of her father who she loved dearly, we had to take her to the doctor, who prescribed her with anti-depression tablets called Prozac. Taking time off of work to look after her, and James doing the same for his mother, we left the business for Percy to run, thinking it was in safe hands, as over the years I had grown to trust him with my life.

Taking a call some weeks later from one of our engineers called Paul, who along with the other engineer had a small percentage of the company, he informed me that he had not been paid his wages for some weeks now. I phoned Percy to tell him what he had said, telling me that there had been a few problems since my being off work, but that he was working through them, and that he would speak to Paul to explain. I thought no more of it, only to get another call the following week from Paul with the same complaints. Turning up at the office one day after making arrangements to meet Percy there, I was told by our office staff that he had phoned in saying that he would not be coming. Thinking it a bit strange that he did not call me direct, I began to feel that something was not quite as it should be. Calling him only to be told that he had been called away on urgent business, and that he would try to meet up with me tomorrow if he could, I could tell by the tone of his voice that something was wrong, saying to him, "Just pop round mine on your way home if you like," as this was my partner who had no problem turning up at my home no matter what the time, only to be told, "I can't make it."

Putting the phone down I asked a member of staff to get me the company books, and phoned a local accountant I had used in the past to come round to my office straight away.

CHAPTER FORTY-THREE

Within ten minutes of going through our company books the accountant looked at me and said, well Tony, I can tell you one thing right off the bat, this company is being eaten alive from the inside out.

Asking him to explain what he meant by that, he proceeded to show me documentation of large withdrawals from the company accounts, and invoices for goods that we had not received. Calling our guy over who dealt with the bank, I asked him to explain these withdrawals, telling me that Percy had been sending him on almost daily basis down to the bank to collect cash for him, informing him that it was to purchase goods for the company, and then he would give him invoices to put in our records. Asking him why he did not notify me of this he said, "Tony if you ask me to do something I don't run it past Percy first, I go ahead and do it, and the same applies to him."

Picking the phone up I called Percy, telling him of what I had found out. He put the phone down without speaking. Two days went by before I was to get a call from Percy. Saying to him, "Look, I don't know what has gone on, but give me any excuse, you have a gambling habit, drug habit, or another woman, and needed the money, tell me you will put the money back and it will all be forgotten, I give you my word," only for him to insist he did not take it. So I replied, "You are telling me that everyone is telling lies on you, and you have not had this money?"

"Yes," he said.

Now this was just adding insult to injury, so telling him he would have to put the money back or there would be serious repercussions, he was to say something to me that made me feel as though I was speaking to a complete stranger on the phone, "Listen," he said, "where do you think I have been for the last two days?"

Telling him I had no idea, he then went on to tell me he had been with a member of a well-known crime family in London and had paid him money, for the purpose of, if anything was to happen to him, to have me shot, and if they couldn't get me, to shoot my son Tony instead. At this time Tony was eight years old. Now I am a man who will deal with anything said or done to me, and this, believe it or not, was not the first time I had been threatened with being shot, but to involve my son in this same sentence, who he had watched grow up, was beyond belief.

"What did you just say?" I replied. "You have just made the biggest mistake of your life mentioning my boy's name. Now I don't want the money back, that option is now closed, you keep it. I think you're going to need it," and slammed the phone down.

Not putting the phone on the hook properly, I could still hear Percy's voice on the other end of the line shouting. Picking it up and listening, I could hear him shouting to someone, "See what you have done? You made me do this, now look at the trouble I am in."

Who was he speaking to? We will never know, but I have my suspicions.

Within hours Percy's cousin called to me, asking if he could see me, telling me that Percy had called him in a terrible state, crying and begging him to help, saying he can't believe what he has said, and wants to apologize and pay the money back, telling him, "I think it has gone a bit too far for that, don't you?"

He asked me, "Please as a personal favor to me, just take the money back and let him go." Agreeing to this, his cousin dropped the money off the next day.

What I wasn't to know was that Percy and David, who had also worked with me both in our previous business selling cars as well as the telecoms venture, had been arrested for importation of goods without paying the relevant duty, and within days our company had gone down the drain.

It was around this time that my eldest daughter Lila Tawny gave birth to my first grandchild, a boy named "James David Russell" born in the St John and Elizabeth Hospital in St John's Wood, London, on the 5th of May 2006.

Some nine months later I was arrested on suspicion of being involved with this crime, as this had apparently been taking place during the time we had worked together. Now it would seem that they had got involved with the bringing in of cigarettes from abroad whilst evading the duty and taxation, and I was arrested for reasons of association, with the charge being conspiracy. Knowing what I know now, the only reason I was arrested and involved in this case was for the fact that Percy wanted me out of the way, and had convinced David to make up a story laying all the blame at my feet, therefore allowing him to walk free. Asking the custom officer in charge on the day of my arrest why I was being arrested and if they thought I was involved, why then had it taken them almost a year to do so, as I was down on the company records as an employee, with my name and address being public knowledge, with him saying, "You should ask your friends that question."

Placing a call to David, asking how this had come about, to my shock and horror he said, "Yes, I am giving evidence against you."

"Why?" I asked. "I have never been anything but a good friend to you, and I can't believe you would do this to me."

Without saying another word he put the phone down. Placing a second call to Percy's brother-in-law Danny telling him of this turn of events, with him saying he would put a call into Percy, to find out what he had to say on the matter, only for him to call me back some minutes later with the message that Percy had said, as he saw it, and I quote, "Every man for himself." Knowing then that I was being fitted up, for a crime I was not involved in but could not get out of, I set my mind to fighting the case with everything I had, to prove my innocence. Finally the day came for the start of the trial, that was to be held in Ipswich Crown Court. Walking into court I was approached by David who said, "Look, I have had a change of heart, and have decided not to give evidence. I hope you can find it in you to forgive me and one day we might be friends again."

Shaking his hand I said, "David, you know I should not be here, and as much as I appreciate, you are not giving evidence against me, it still does not make this problem go away, but thank you anyway."

Now he said, "I better let Percy know."

Walking over to where Percy and his sons were sitting, David proceeded to tell them of his decision. With Percy unable to contain his anger I watched as he tried to convince David to follow through with his plan, for what I did not realize was that not only did this throw a spanner in the works of the prosecution, but Percy, who was relying on David giving his evidence that it was all my doing, had not even prepared a defense. So entering court for the start of the trail, Percy's defense barrister stood up and asked for the trial to be halted as his client had all of a sudden been brought down with a severe migraine, and would not be able to fully comprehend what was going on. With the judge ruling in his favor, and allowing him two days to recover, the trial was rescheduled to start the following week. Monday morning came and with it the swearing in of the jury.

Taking my place in the dock, along with ten others, some known to me and some I had never seen before, with two of the defendants taking this opportunity to plead guilty and not go through with the trail, that left eight of us. As is the case with most trials, they start with telling the jury what we are charged with and the background of the case, and the case was that a system was set up within the docks, that would allow these men to bring goods in from Russia on a container ship, have it unloaded and take it out of the docks without any checks. Of all the evidence they had, the only so-called link to me was that they had a camera recording of a meeting with me and one of the other defendants, and that one of the other people involved in the case had a telephone with the initial "T" in it – that was it – and of course the prosecution were saying the meeting was to discuss this illegal business, and the "T" in the phone stood for "Tony". Sitting in the dock day after day while the prosecution went through their evidence for the first six weeks, finally the time came for us to make our defense opening statements, with me being defended by Mr. Jonathon Woodcock QC, and all the defendants having their own barristers.

The day came for each of us defendants to take the stand to give our version of events, in order of being indicted. With David refusing to take the stand and give evidence, it then passed on to Percy. Taking his place in the witness box it very soon became apparent that he was in no way near prepared for it, as let's face it, he had only the last weekend to prepare, and with hundreds of pages of statements, along with untold amounts of exhibits, he was soon lost, telling the prosecution that he worked on a part-time basis for the telecoms company, and that he traveled to and from his home near Chertsey in Surrey to Harlow in Essex, three days a week by train to carry out this work. Asking him to tell the court the route he took on an almost daily basis by train, he was unable to, saying he had forgot.

"OK," the prosecutor said, "what about how much it costs you to buy the ticket for this journey?" Again he could not recall. "So," said the prosecutor, "you are telling this court that you make a trip two to three times a week by train, for nearly two years, and you can't tell us the route, i.e. what station in London you go to, what train you then change to for the second part of this trip to Harlow, or even how much the ticket costs?"

"No," replied Percy.

"Why?" said the prosecutor.

"I forgot," said Percy.

"You forgot! A trip you are telling us you have taken hundreds of times, and you forgot. I put it to you that you have not forgot, but are telling lies to this court Mr. Smith." And so this was the pattern of questioning throughout Percy's evidence, time and time again being caught out, with no attention to detail.

Next up was Martin Easterbrook, known to me as I had met him before to discuss the supply of fencing timber, of which he had a company within the docks that imported the raw wood for this purpose. This was the man whom I had met on the occasion we were filmed together. In going through the evidence I had found a statement with several pieces blanked out, made by this man. After showing it to David we decided to ask our barristers to make an application to have this statement opened so as we could see what he had said. After some argument that we were within our rights to know what was being withheld from us, it turns out that during an interview, this man had asked that the police place a wire on him for the purpose of having a meeting with his co-accused and that he would try and entrap them into making a statement of their guilt.

After some weeks it was my turn to take the stand. For three days I was asked in great detail to explain my part in this turn of events, then it was the turn of our council to put forward our defense, with me calling several witnesses to speak on my behalf, who gave evidence to the fact that I had approached them for the purpose of selling them the timber which I was to purchase from this man's company.

After eleven weeks finally the trial was over and all that was left to do was for the judge to give his summing up of events and send the jury out for their deliberations. Three days went by, and then we were to get the news they had come up with some verdicts. Taking our places in the dock, they came back with guilty verdicts on David and Percy. With the judge thanking them for their verdict he sent them back into their room to carry on with the job of reaching a verdict on the remainder of us accused, thinking to myself that as far as I was concerned things had gone well for me throughout the trial, but that you can never see how people are thinking and how the jury had taken in my evidence. This I have to say was one of the most stressful times of my life, knowing that the twelve people in that jury room held, in a sense, my life and future in their hands, knowing that if found guilty I would most certainly be sentenced to many years in prison.

The following morning we were brought back into court for to hear the jury's verdicts, with this man Martin Easterbrook also being found guilty along with one of the other defendants; then again two days later calling us back in to hear that three of the other men in the case had been found not guilty. This left me the last man standing, and after several more days, finally I was called into court to hear the jury's decision.

CHAPTER FORTY-FOUR

Asking me to stand, and then asking the foreman of the jury to stand, the clerk to the court asked the question, "Foreman of the jury, have you reached a verdict on the defendant Antony Eugene Marshall?"

"No your honor," the foreman replied, with the judge asking him, "If I were to give you more time, do you think it is within your powers as a jury to do so?" – only for the foreman to reply, "No your honor, we do not think that is possible."

So, a Hung Jury. Thinking that was the end of my ordeal, the judge after a brief exchange of words with the prosecutor decided as was within their powers to go for a re-trial, of me on my own, and as I was neither found neither guilty nor not guilty was allowed to go free. Now this was not the ideal turn of events, but it was a whole lot better than being found guilty, and I was happy to at least be going home with my wife and kids.

With the words of my barrister being, "Well at least we live to fight another day," ringing in my ears, I left court. Returning some weeks later to attend the sentencing of my co-accused, I sat and watched as the judge handed down sentences of seven and a half years to Percy, David and the other defendants. This, even though I had fallen out with them big time, did not give me any sense of pleasure, for in my opinion I would not put my worst enemy in prison, and only felt sorry for their families.

With the date being set for my re-trial, I again set about going over every detail of the last trial, examining every piece of evidence, exhibit, and statement that was available to me, also all the new evidence that had been provided for this new trial. Coming across a statement that was within the new bundles, I called and asked to see my defense solicitor. The new trial date was set and was to come around very soon.

In between trials one of my twins, Jade, came to me saying she wanted to get married, as she had fallen in love with a boy by the name of Billy Clayden. She had only been going out with this boy for a short period of time, and it came as quite a shock to us, as me and Lila had not even met him. Saying she did not want a big wedding as Billy had lost his father a few years before, and did not want it to be a big occasion, we agreed. Coming into my home for the first time Billy instantly felt like one of the family, and after putting their bands in they were married on the 17th of November 2007 in Epping Register Office, my birthday, with the reception being held in a friend of mine's restaurant called the Piano Lounge in Epping. As I have said previously, giving your daughter to be married is in my opinion one of the hardest things a man can do, with worries of are you doing the right thing. And at least with my eldest daughter's wedding we had plenty of time to adjust to the situation, but this happened so quick, that I have no shame in saying I woke up the next morning, and on seeing her bedroom empty, cried like a child for my loss. But I have to say that Jade and Billy have made a great life together, and all my worries were unfounded.

Finally the trial date came, being met by my barrister on the steps of the courthouse, he said, "Are we ready for round two Tony?" Nodding my head to him he said, "Well let's go 'em."

Once again taking my place in the dock, but this time on my own, I felt a sense of relief as this time I only had my own evidence to contend with, and would not be weighed down with the silly mistakes of my co-accused, also armed with the statement I had found, I felt more than confident that the truth would out. The first trial lasted eleven weeks, with eleven defendants; this trial lasted nine weeks on my own, after hearing all the evidence and my witnesses once again coming forward to speak in my defense.

With the judge having to take another hearing one day, I was allowed the day off to spend at home, with Lila Tawny due any day to have her second child. This it would seem was fate, as James was working away at the time. First thing in the morning, Lila would pop in and see how she was doing; coming back she said to me, Lila Tawny was getting a few pains, and even though it was a bit early, I had better get ready in case we needed to take her to the hospital in Romford. Coming back up, only this time in a state of panic, Lila said, "The baby is coming; we have to take her now."

Jumping in my car with Lila Tawny, her mother, sister Amber and Grandmother Zenda, we sped off en route to Romford and the hospital she was booked into, but this was by now 8 in the morning and rush hour traffic; making it to Romford but stuck in heavy traffic, Lila Tawny declared, "Dad get me to the hospital NOW!!"

Pulling up alongside an ambulance I told the driver that my girl was having a baby and could he please get me through this traffic. He replied, "I can't mate, I have a patient in the back."

Jumping the lights and driving the wrong way down the road into oncoming traffic, flashing my lights to make the cars pull over out of my way, the ambulance driver must have thought he had better come to my assistance, or we would all be killed. Following me he overtook and with lights and sirens blaring guided us into the hospital car park. Rushing Lila Tawny in to the maternity wing, she was taken into a room and five minutes later my second grandson was born, "Joseph John Russell", some two weeks early, so as I said having the day off was fated.

Finally the day arrived when at the end of the trial the head officer in charge takes to the stand to give his evidence and opinion as to the case, with the prosecutor once again going over his evidence that there was no one else involved in this case known to him with a name beginning with the letter "T", and that in his expert opinion the phone that was found with this initial "T" in it was for a number that was somehow linked to me. "Yes," he replied.

"Well your Honor and Ladies and Gentlemen of the Jury, I rest my case."

Now it was our turn to ask the questions of this officer of the points he had made. Picking up the statement I had found within the bundles and turning to look at me before turning his attention to the chief officer, my barrister Mr. Woodcock asked, "If I can just go back to the final question put to you by my learned friend the prosecutor, that throughout your most stringent investigation of this case, there is or was, no one else known to you in the whole of your inquiries, by the name that begins with the letter 'T'?"

"Yes," replied the officer.

"You're sure of this?" asked Mr. Woodcock.

"Yes I am positive," came the reply.

"Well then can I please draw your attention to a statement taken some months ago?" – asking him to locate it within the file holders that were placed upon the witness stand. "Found it?" asked Mr. Woodcock.

"Yes," replied the officer.

"OK good," said my barrister, "could you please read out loud so as the jury can hear you, the sentence beginning with 'And I met…', about halfway down page number two."

Finding this, the officer looked as if he had seen a ghost, and looked towards the prosecutor.

"Don't look at my learned friend," said my barrister, "I am afraid he can't help you now. Please read out the lines of this statement as instructed, in a loud voice if you will so as the jury can hear."

Starting to read he said, "And I met on two occasions a man known to me as Tony Marshall, who was involved with Percy and David in the telecoms business, this man I would describe as..." Going on, he gave a brief description of me, then he said, "I also met on another occasion a further man who was introduced to me as 'T'. Thinking this was a strange name I asked him what the 'T' stood for, and was told his name was Tom but everyone called him 'T'."

Asking him if he could read the name on the bottom of this statement as to the person who took down this statement he said, "Yes," and read out the name.

"And would you mind telling the jury who that is?" asked my barrister.

"Me," came the reply.

"Yes you," said Mr. Woodcock, "but you have just given evidence that there was no one else known to you within the whole of your investigations by the name 'T'. How can this be?"

"I forgot," came the reply.

"You forgot the most important piece of evidence that there was someone else involved called 'T' in this case. The one piece of evidence that proves that my client may not be the person you are looking for and you forgot it."

On hearing this, the jury had a look of utter disbelief on their faces and after giving them a few more points to contend with, the judge sent them out to deliberate. For nine days they stayed out debating, with once every morning and evening, me taking my place in the stand, while the jury was called in for to be asked if they had come to a verdict. After nine days, finally they sent word that they had come to a decision and after once again standing up to be asked if they had come to a verdict, the foreman of the jury said "No your Honor we have not."

Again being asked if he was to give them more time, did they think they could reach one, only to be told, "No your Honor we do not." Another Hung Jury.

Excusing the jury the judge once again spoke with the prosecutor, saying, "Do we go again?" With the prosecutor stating, "Your Honor, we have no further evidence available that would warrant the cost of a further trial, and therefore it is the opinion of the prosecution that we leave it at that."

Looking at me the judge said, "You may go."

That was it: no apology, no sorry for wasting your time. But I didn't care, for as far as I was concerned, the terrible ordeal for me, Lila and my family was over. Leaving the court house I gathered all of us into a group hug, and after shaking the hands of my lawyer Richard Block and barrister Jonathon Woodcock, we headed off to the pub to celebrate, being joined later by a member of the jury who said that all the other members had been waiting in another pub down the road in the hope we would be coming there, and had now gone home. And on asking her how they had come up with the hung jury, she said it was nine to two in favor of a not guilty verdict with one member abstaining from the vote, therefore causing the hung jury. Thanking her and asking her to please thank the other members, we said our goodbyes and headed home.

Waking up the next morning I felt as if I was having a nervous breakdown, and could not stop shaking. Getting a call from Clare who worked for my solicitors, she asked, "How are you feeling?"

"Not too good in actual fact," I said.

"That's why I have called," she went on to say. "You see, Tony, your brain has been working overtime to fight this case, and now you are suffering from the comedown. We see this all the time with our clients; what you need is a good holiday to get over it."

Thanking her for the call and all of her assistance in my trials, I put the phone down. Within two days I was on a beach in Mexico.

Recently I have heard a rumor that this man Martin Easterbrook was to meet one of the Frankhams in Ford Prison, and on hearing my name being mentioned, had said I was the person who had made the statement as to wearing the wire. Well, what follows is an actual transcript of the statement that has been supplied to me by my solicitor, it is information that is public record, and as such is very easy to validate and authenticate: I have marked out the section that was covered up in the original discloser.

	It was timber I'm known for that I'm fucking good at it so at the end of the day whatever conjecture or theory you've caught me on tape yes it doesn't look good.
LANE	Hmm.
EASTABROOK	I'm not fucking stupid.
LANE	No.
EASTABROOK	I know whether I spend twenty years in prison or not I'm not an unintelligent guy and as far as I'm, I'm cool. If you want I will wear a wire tape these guys up for you and get them to admit their involvement or not.
LANE	Yeah.
EASTABROOK	Yes if that's what it takes to prove my innocence or not I will do it
LANE	Are you saying this is something you would be prepared to do.
EASTABROOK	Yeah I don't even know these guys.
LANE	Okay.
EASTABROOK	I mean as I have said I'm not involved in this and I'm not going back to prison for no one.
LANE	Okay well if you've nothing further.
EASTABROOK	No.
LANE	I've nothing further right in that case it's 17:03 hours and I'll terminate the interview.

So you people that were sitting, listening and feeding cups of tea to this person while he called me a grass, were in actual fact sitting, listening and feeding cups of tea "to a Grass". Fools, you should be wise enough and old enough to know me better than that.

CHAPTER FORTY-FIVE

After having a few weeks in Cancun and Disney World with Lila and my boys Tony and Santino, I felt like I had washed away all of the stress and strains of the trials. Returning home I carried on life as normal, buying and selling cars.

With two of my girls now married and living on my land in Essex, it came the time for the christening of my grandson James, having him christened in the Abbey where she was married, with Lila's brother James and his wife Zoe being among the godparents. All was going well until my nephew Jim turned up, having not been invited by Lila Tawny and James, for accusing James of trying to break into his car some weeks before. Walking out I asked him to come in and shake hands with James and that would be the end of it. He refused, and instead of coming in he asked his granny and uncles to leave with him, with his aunt Lila coming out to say, "You should not have said what you did about James, come and shake his hand and be friends and forget about it."

He would not listen, so with all of Lila Tawny's family walking out except us, this put a bad light on the festivities, with people asking what was wrong. We made the best of a bad situation and enjoyed the rest of the day.

Seeing Jim pull onto our camp the next day Lila walked down to speak with Jim, saying, "Why did you do what you did yesterday? That was embarrassing, for your cousin."

One word followed the next, with Lila and her mother exchanging words. Walking down, I pulled Lila away, saying, "Leave it, let it go," thinking I would take her home and that things would calm down. With Lila still having heated words with her mother that she should not have walked out of the reception, Lila's brother James pushed her. Saying to him, "Don't push her," he drew back and threw a punch at me, missing.

I stepped back and said, "What are you doing, div (fool)?" thinking this was done in a moment's madness, and he would regain his senses and stop. For what you have to realize is, this young man was as close as a son to me, and I could no more fight with him, than my own son, and if I was to do so and lay a hand on him, I could not have lived with myself, until I cut the hand off that I had used against him.

Again he stepped forward and threw another punch. Shouting, "Now, that's enough, I won't fight you," and with everyone else now running forward to stop it, I looked at him and said, "How could you try and hit me? I have loved you like a son, how dare you do this to me?"

At this point my nephew Jim Brazil ran up behind me and punched me in the back of my head. Turning to him I said, "You fucking monkey."

Running from me he ran up James's trailer and shouted, "Give me a knife," with my daughter Amber stood there. What she said: "A knife to use on my father, you fucking coward. My father who has been like your own. Get out," she said, "you won't be stabbing my dad today," being pulled away from each other by the rest of the family.

I was in a state of shock at what had just happened. Reaching the door of my home, I said, "I don't believe you lot, after all these years I have put into you, you have the audacity to treat me like this, me of all people."

Running back down to where I was standing, Jim shouted, "I am the man for you, fight me," beating his hand on his chest.

"You fight me you snot box?" I replied. "You're having a fucking laugh, ain't you?"

With everyone pulling them away from my door, I looked at them and said, "You should be ashamed of yourselves, how dare you want to fight with me? Now fuck off away from my door and don't ever look in my direction again, we are finished."

Later that day I was to get a call from a very good friend of mine, asking if I was OK. Saying, "Yes I am fine why?" – thinking, "What has he heard?"

He was to tell me that my nephew Jim had been round his place telling him that him and James had beaten me so badly that an ambulance had to be called, and I was so injured they had to roll me onto the stretcher, that they had broken nearly every bone in my body, and I would be lucky to survive, with my good friend saying to Jim, "If that is the case Jim you have knocked me sick, for I know how much Tony thought of you both."

Telling my friend, "I can't believe what they have done," but that the only thing they had broken was my heart, he was unable to talk anymore. I could hear his voice breaking as he said goodbye, for he knew how much I bestowed in these young men and just how much I was hurting inside. To think I had half-raised these people and been through so much with them, never leaving them in times of need, and this was the thanks I got. Days, weeks and months went by with us not speaking, both going our separate ways in life.

Getting a call from my mother one day she said my father had been taken into hospital having suffered another stroke and we had better come, reaching the hospital and speaking to the doctors, who told me that my father had suffered a major stroke this time, and it had affected his swallow, making it impossible to eat food for fear he may choke, but that they were feeding him intravenously until such time as they worked on getting it working again. But it soon became apparent that this stroke was a bridge too far for my father to cross, with the doctors now having to inject liquid food into his stomach to keep him alive. Gathering us together one day after weeks in the hospital, the doctors told us there was nothing more they could do for him.

Asking my mother to get a priest to come see him, my father asked him to read him his last rights. With the priest asking if my father wanted him to hear his confession, I said, "How long did you say you have, Father Kennedy?" – making my father and the priest laugh.

Later that day we took my father home. Now basically it was only the fact that my father could not eat, as with his weak swallow the fear was it going down into his lungs instead of his stomach, and with the injections not working, it was literally a case that he would starve to death.

After some days of watching him suffer, with the doctors coming out on a daily basis, I spoke to them about how he was suffering and if there was something that could be done to put him out of this long and torturous way of dying. Telling me that they could give him a morphine patch that on top of the amounts he had in his system for the pain, would cause an overdose, and he would just slip away in peace, but that by law they could not administer the patch, but could give it to a member of the family to do so.

After speaking with my mother, brother Lee and sisters, I went to speak with my father, telling him the truth that he was going to have to suffer a long and painful death, and of the morphine option, he looked at me and said, "Do it." Asking if he was sure he nodded his head and said, "I have had enough."

Telling the doctor of my father's decision, it was agreed she would deliver the patch to us the following morning. That night I never slept a minute wondering if I was doing the right thing, but I came to the decision that if the shoe was on the other foot, I would want to take this option, and go out with my dignity intact, knowing the things that were happening to my father and how his body was shutting down, was not a way he would want to leave this earth, being the proud man he was. So it was agreed I would be the one to carry out the task of placing this patch on my father. Going in to speak with my father again, I asked him if he was still sure about his decision. "Yes," he said, once again telling me he had had enough, so sitting him up in the bed, we sat and spoke, telling him how much I loved him and would always love him, and asking if he knew this.

He reached out and took my hand and smiled at me. Cuddling him I kissed him on the cheek and placed the morphine patch on the back of his shoulder. With the tears now streaming down my face I said, You rest now and I will see you soon." Nodding his head he laid back and drifted into a sleep. That evening he passed away.

While sitting with him for those last few hours, I thought back on all the things he had done in his lifetime, the places he had seen, and of how he had raised us children, making me the man I am today; remembering of how he had loaned me a thousand pounds towards the buying of my first car, telling me, "This is not a gift, but a loan which I want paid back as soon as possible, understand," installing a work ethic in me from such a tender age, that still beats there to this day; of how he had left a mark on so many people, for he was known throughout the world among Gypsy people; a strict father and hard taskmaster at times but always there for us in times of need.

We buried him in Rose Hill Cemetery in Doncaster, where my brother John was cremated, next to where a tree was planted in his memory from his ex-wife. There is not a day goes by that I don't think of him or bring him up in a conversation, for he was, and will be forever more, one of my heroes.

After spending a few days with my mother to make sure she was OK, we returned back to our home in Essex, and with me carrying on with the buying and selling of cars, I was approached by another Gypsy man by the name of Jesse Richards, who I had known for some years as he was the cousin of my brother-in-law Jim Brazil, who had died some years earlier, asking if I would be interested in buying his cars. After placing his cars with a dealer friend of mine so as I was to get a drink out of the deal, while delivering them we got to talking, with Jesse telling me he had to sell them as he had a property business venture he was setting up, and was in need of the funds. Asking if I would be interested in loaning him an amount of which he would pay good interest on, we struck a deal. Telling him he would have to put something up as security against the loan, he told me this would not be a problem, and that he would sign a piece of land he owned over to me until such time as he re-paid the loan.

Agreeing this, and on receipt of confirmation the land was in my name, I loaned him the amount he was asking for. What I did not know was that Jesse had loaned money from quite a few other people, and was not paying off the interest on time, and the other people were involved with my brother-in-law James.

Phoning me one day Jesse was to mention the problems he was having in keeping up to speed with his payments, telling him, "Look, don't worry about paying me this month, get these other people sorted out and off your back, then we can work out my bit, OK?" Agreeing this, he put the phone down.

This was the last time I was to speak to Jesse again, for after turning up to a meeting with James and the other people who were owed money, an argument took place, that led to a fight, with Jesse coming off the worst, with the people who were owed the money putting Jesse in a vehicle and taking him away. He was never to be seen again.

Now in my opinion, the only crime my brothers-in-law were to commit, was being in the wrong place at the wrong time, with inexperienced people who could not handle the situation, and for being too loyal and upstanding of men. Jesse's body has never been recovered. Questions are being asked from his family, but these questions are being asked of the wrong people.

James was to go on the run, with a nationwide police search taking place as to his whereabouts, with *Crimewatch* running a segment asking the public for information that may lead to his arrest. Some months later he was to be arrested in Blackpool and is now serving eighteen years for manslaughter.

CHAPTER FORTY-SIX

By now my son Tony Jr was ten years old. Picking him up from school one day, he came out with a strange look on his face. Asking him what was wrong he proceeded to tell me that he had been involved in a fight in the playground over another boy calling him a pikey, and that he thought he had killed him. Stopping the car, I said, "What? Tell me exactly what happened."

It turns out that after few words this boy came running to try and punch him. Telling me how he ducked under this boy's punch and threw a right hand back, catching this boy on the chin and as it would seem knocked him spark out, telling me of how this boy lay motionless apart from his knees shaking, and that his eyes had rolled back white, I could see by the look on my son's face that he truly believed he had killed this boy. Explaining to him that the boy was only knocked out, and that when we got home we would have his mother call the school to see how he was, telling him that he did the right thing, as all my children were taught not to start a fight, but if someone tries to hit you, make sure you hit back.

After this it seemed that Tony had become the boy to beat, with not a day going by he was in some sort of fight or another, so I decided it was time to take him boxing to make sure if he was going to fight he knew what he was doing, so taking him along to the local boxing club called the Hoddesdon Boxing Academy. After buying him some gloves and a headguard, he took to it like a duck to water, with me telling him I just wanted him to train for the first few weeks, and not to spar until he felt ready, but to my amazement, as soon as we walked in, the trainer said, "Whoever wants to spar get in the ring."

No sooner had he said the words then Tony was in the ring. Walking over to Sab Leo, the head coach of the club, I said, "Sab, I don't really want him to spar, as this is the first time he has ever set foot in a boxing ring."

Assuring me that he would look after him and make sure the boys took it easy on him, I agreed to see how it went for a round or two. With Tony sparring one boy and then another, Sab turned to me and said, "Don't look so worried. If this is the first time he has sparred, he is one of the best natural talents I have ever seen."

After a few months of training the time came for Tony to have his first proper bout, getting matched with a boy from Finchley who had already boxed three times, losing one. With Tony losing on a majority verdict, the bout was very close, and I thought Tony had done enough to win, but with the boy being from the local club he got the decision. On the way home I can't tell you how upset Tony was: looking at me he said, "I thought I won that fight Dad."

"So do I, son," I replied, "but what you have to do, is take it out of the judges' hands next time. Don't give them any excuses, or an opportunity to give the verdict the other way. Win and win big."

Nodding his head in agreement, he went on to win his next ten fights in a row, beating some of the best young boys in the country. I cannot put into words how proud I am of how he handled himself in his boxing, with me taking a hands-on role in the training of the boys, becoming one of the trainers, bringing into effect some of the circuit training I had learned in prison. We had a fantastic squad, with some of the boys going on to win the ABA Finals, and representing England in the Three Nations.

In the summer of 2009 we were invited to the wedding of the daughter of good friends of ours, Albert and Omi Douglas, in Dubai. I had flown in and out of Dubai in transit to Australia on a few occasions, but never actually spent any time there as such, and if I am honest it was never a place that had jumped off the map as a holiday destination. But with me, Lila and my daughter Amber coming along to the wedding that was to be held at the Mina A'Salam Hotel on the Jumeirah Beach, I was to be pleasantly shocked by this wonderful country and its people.

After spending four glorious days, the time came for us to return. Coming home I now knew how Lila had felt all those years before on returning to Surrey, what with all that had gone on with me and her family. It just didn't feel the same anymore, so after a few weeks, we decided to take a trip back to Dubai, this time with our two sons, with thoughts of setting up a construction company, and hopefully spending a little time there.

Within months I was off and running, setting up a company and winning several large contracts. After renting an apartment on the Palm Jumeirah, we settled into our new life in the UAE. Spending time in the company of the locals, I found it amazing how similar we were in our thoughts and way of life. I think this affinity I feel towards these people stems from our own ancestry, being of Egyptian heritage, with their old-fashioned and respectful ways towards their elders and love of their children.

I feel that if Gypsies were to have their own country and government, it would be just like this. The way they look after their own, is something to be admired, with them striving to lead the way in everything they do, wanting it to be the biggest and best, no matter what; their acceptance of others as long as you are prepared to pull your weight, with no freeloaders putting a tax on the economy, and speaking of tax, the word does not exist in Dubai. The first thing that hit me was how clean the place was, with not so much as a matchstick to be found on the streets, and the service in the hotels and restaurants being second to none. With alcohol and drugs being frowned on, there are no drunks or junkies walking around. Never in my life have I seen a safer place to bring up children, for the police are very strict and crack down on any illegal activity almost before it takes place.

With us traveling back and forth from the UK so as to spend some time with our children and grand kids, of which we had a new addition, with my daughter Jade giving birth to our first granddaughter, "Shakira Marshall Clayden", born on the 6th October 2009, beautiful beyond belief and has her mother and grandmother's personality to the tee, also spending time with our two daughters who were still at home, as they were courting and did not want to be so far away from their boyfriends, also taking turns to come have a few weeks with us in Dubai, life was good. With both girls getting engaged and setting their dates within a month of each other, soon it came time to travel back for the weddings, both to be held in the Walled Garden Pavilion, Hanbury Manor, Hertfordshire, with Montana being the first to tie the knot, to Joe Gaskin from Doncaster. I know what you're thinking: he is a distant cousin of Joe Boy, his family have been friends of ours for years, and he is one of the nicest people you could meet, who worships the ground my daughter walks on, so I could not ask for anything more.

May 7th 2011 will stay with me forever, as my girl looked beautiful, the weather was perfect and so was the company, with all in attendance having a wonderful time. Walking her down the aisle of Waltham Abbey is one of my proudest moments as a father, and one of the funniest moments being while making my speech that I had prepared, an old friend of mine Jim Barr shouted, “Don’t read, just wing it,” only for me to reply, “The last time I tried to wing it, I nearly got seven and a half years,” making everyone laugh.

Now came Amber’s special day, with Amber marrying Lila’s cousin Joe Boy Botton’s son Narny, whom she had been going out with since being 16 years old. June 10th was another wonderful day, spent with all of our fantastic friends and family, again walking down the aisle of the Abbey, to the sounds of Celine Dion playing in the background. Seeing the look of love on Amber and Narny’s faces as they said their vows, moments like these I feel stay with you for the rest of your life, then on to the reception, with the meals being prepared by Ashby of London catering company, and string quartets playing on the lawn, it came time for the speeches, with another speech having a profound effect on the guests, that of Ambers twin sister Jade, telling of how they had shared their lives together, how she was her twin, her other half, and how much she loved her, bringing everyone to tears. Taking the floor with my girls for our dance, I can’t tell you how proud I was of what beautiful young women they had become, and at the end, I remember cuddling them and telling them how much I love and always will love them, and that they will always be my babies.

I said in my speech at Amber’s wedding, that if my daughters had asked me to go out and find them husbands, I could not have done a better job, for not only are they my son-in-laws, but some of my closest friends and confidants, and I feel very lucky to call them so.

Returning back to Dubai shortly after the weddings, Montana, Joe and Amber and Narny came over to spend a few months with us. Going to work in the week and spending the weekends on the beach or around the pool, then heading off to the shopping malls in the evenings, these were wonderful days. Taking them to our favorite restaurants and bars and just spending time with them as married people was great, for if I am honest, me and my girls did not always see eye to eye on a lot of topics, with me being at times Public Enemy No. 1for being a bit overly strict with them, not allowing them to go many places. But I think as they have gotten older, they have come to realize that I was only trying to protect them from the big bad world that’s out there, and now we have so much more than a father-child relationship: we are friends first, they can come to me and talk about anything, and value my opinion as I value theirs, for not only have my daughters grown into beautiful young women, they have a wisdom and viewpoint well beyond their young years.

With both girls returning home to the UK, they phoned us with the news they were both expecting within a few weeks of each other, and with Jade giving birth to her second child any time we flew home for the birth. Baby Billy was born in Harlow, Essex, on the 28th March 2013, one of the most handsome babies I have ever set eyes on.

Again returning back to Dubai a few weeks later, as over the last four years it had truly become our home, I was to get a phone call from my eldest sister Linda one day. As soon as she came on the phone I instantly knew something was wrong from the sound of her voice. "What is it," I asked, "what's happened?"

With her voice cracking she went on to tell me that she had taken my mother to the hospital, as she had developed a rash on her breast and after a visit to the doctor he had made her an appointment with a specialist. After being checked over the specialist had informed her she had breast cancer. Hearing the words cancer and my mother in the same sentence I have to tell you my world came to a crashing halt, for it seemed as though time was standing still, almost as if I was in a bad dream. Only when Linda spoke again asking if I could hear her did I snap back to reality.

"What?" I said. "Say that again," as if refusing to believe what I had just heard.

She replied, "I am sorry Tony to tell you like this over the phone but I knew you would want to know straight away, my Mam has got breast cancer."

Asking her if the doctor was sure of this, she said, "They are going to do some tests, but the specialist is more than sure it's cancer." Asking to speak to my mother, who on hearing my voice broke down into tears, I tried to speak but the words would not come out.

Putting the phone down I cried like a child, then as always in times like this something kicked in, an inner voice that tells me you have to be strong for everyone, that she is relying on your being strong and depending on your strength. Gathering myself I called my mother back, telling her not to worry, that I would be on the next flight home, and who knows doctors have made mistakes before, but whatever the outcome we would deal with it, if it's cancer we will fight it, reminding her of how strong of a woman she was, and that she had dealt with everything that life had thrown in her direction up till now, and that she had always came back fighting.

"Yes," she said, "Tony, you're right."

Putting the phone down I felt gutted, for at this point my mother was 80 years old, and had been through so much heartache in her lifetime, that just when it seemed she was going to live out the rest of her life in happiness, and had put so much pain behind her, something like this could happen.

Arriving home and traveling straight up to Doncaster, we took my mother to have the biopsy tests done, with the results coming back that she did have a strong form of cancer and in the specialist's opinion her breast and lymph nodes would have to be removed as soon as possible. Asking the doctor what he thought the chances were of my mother making it through such a big operation, he replied, "If I did not think your mother was strong enough to deal with the operation I would say so, but apart from the cancer your mother is one of the fittest and strongest woman for her age I have ever come across, and I have no concerns as to her going through the op and making a full recovery."

Coming out of the doctor's office, we went for a cup of tea, and along with the rest of the family we sat down to talk. Looking at my mother, I asked, "What do you want to do Mam, for at the end of the day it has to be your decision, but in my opinion I would have the surgery and hopefully that will be the end of it."

After speaking with all of us, she made her mind up that she would have the operation. After informing the doctor to make the arrangements, we took her home. Within days a date was set, and booking her in to the private wing of Doncaster Royal Infirmary, she went down to have her surgery. After several hours that seemed like years, she came back up to her room, and meeting with the surgeon he informed us that the operation was a success and as far as he was concerned, they had removed all of the cancerous cells. Taking my mother home, I thanked God that it looked as if she could now put this behind her, but that was not to be the end of this nightmare.

Taking my mother back some months later for a scan, the doctor informed her that they most have missed some of the cells and her cancer had returned. This would require her to have to undergo extensive chemotherapy for several months. Now this is not an easy thing for a young woman to go through, and as strong as she was it really took its toll on my mother, with the side-effects being the loss of her hair. I was heartbroken for her, knowing how proud my mother was of her looks, as she has always looked after herself, making sure her hair and makeup was done to perfection, even if only going out to the local shop, and along with the ill feeling that comes with the chemo, it was just too much for her to take. So the decision was made that rather then put herself through any more of this form of torture, she would have a further operation to go in and remove the remainder of the cancer, this time having the operation in Guildford as she had been living with my sister Romain in Surrey. With most of her children and grandchildren there, they took her down again. Coming out from the surgery she looked amazing, making sure she had her wig on before anyone saw her. Once again we crossed our fingers that this time they had got the last of the cancer. All we could do was wait until her next check-up and scan to see the results. Returning some weeks later the doctors told her that as far as they could see, they had got it all and it all seemed clear. Finally some good news, but this was to be short-lived.

Some weeks later my mother developed a rash on her arms and back, and after a trip back to her specialist, they told her the cancer had spread into her system, and after a meeting with the top doctors involved, they have decided to put her on to a new treatment, that in the whole of the country there is only a handful of patients who qualify for it. So going once a month for this treatment, she seems as though she is beating this horrible disease. I pray to God she does. Telling me if she could just have a few more years she would be happy, and every time she says it I die a little more inside, for if anyone deserves a bit of happiness in their lives it is her, after putting up with so much in life, having to bury two of her children as youngsters; I can't imagine the pain of this, but even though she is going through this terrible time, never once has she complained. Whenever I speak with her she is full of concern for everyone else but her, one of the bravest people I know, a better mother a person could not ask for. I pray to God she pulls through this, for I am not ready to say goodbye to her, my mother: *another one of my heroes in life*.

CHAPTER FORTY-SEVEN

Leaving my mother in the care of my sisters, we traveled back once again to Dubai, carrying on from where I had left off. With my business here going from strength to strength, I could not ask for anything more, with Montana giving birth to a boy "Joseph James Antony Santino" on the 5th May 2013, born several weeks early but he has grown into a beautiful bouncing boy, who I adore, and Amber having a baby girl "Amber Jade Lila Montana" on the 2nd of June 2013, who is her grandmother re-born apart from having my blue eyes: truly beautiful.

Life has dealt me a fair hand, with a few hiccups along the way, with my oldest son Tony turning into a clone of my brother John, not just in his good looks but in his nature. It is as though I have my brother back once again, for not only is Tony my son but my best friend. He is going through those difficult teenage years at present where we don't always see eye to eye, and he seems to have a different viewpoint on most things we discuss, but he is and always will be my firstborn son.

Santino is the brains of the family. At nine years of age he can hold conversations with adults that can't help but leave them impressed, and in so many ways he is a miniature version of myself, not just in looks, but in his outlook on life. I think of myself as being truly blessed to have such a wonderful family, seeing my children grow into fine young men and women.

For this past four years I have been a resident of Dubai and in a sense it feels like home to me, with the only hardship being so far away from those we love. If I could somehow transport all the people we care about over to be with us I would be in no great hurry to return to the UK, and with the children regularly taking turns to come and spend time with us, and us trying to get back as often as we can, it seems to be working out OK, but in the words of Dorothy from *The Wizard of Oz*, "There's no place like home", and home is and forever will be England.

Well, this is the end of my story. I hope you have enjoyed hearing some of the tales of mine and my families past. When my father was alive I lost count of the times I said to him, "You should write a book about your life," and sadly he never got the chance, but I hope my accounts have done justice to his memory.

Glossary of some Romany Words

Akai	Here
Aladged	Ashamed
Amoni	Anvil
Arvah	Yes
Avree	Away
Bal/Val	Hair
Bar	A pound sterling
Barri	Good
Bashadi	A Fiddle
Bokht	Bad Luck/Fortune
Bokra	Sheep
Bori	Large
Bourlo	Pig/Swine
Bourlo Mass	Pork
Bul	Rump/Buttock
Butsi/Butty	Work
Canni	Hen
Catches	Scissors
Chavi	Child
Chingring	Quarrelling/Arguing
Chitchi	Nothing
Choka/s	Shoe/Shoes
Chop	Exchange
Chordi	Stolen
Chore	Steal/Thief
Coor	Fight
Cooroboshno	A fighting Cock
Coover	Thing
Cosht	Stick
Dai	Father
Danyer/s	Tooth/Teeth
Deek	Look
Deeking	Looking
Del	Hit/Give
Dickler	Neckscarf

Dinnelo	**A Fool**
Dinneloness	**Foolishness**
Divi	**Mad**
Divvus	**Day**
Dordie	**Exclamation**
Drom	**Road**
Dui	**Two**
Dukker	**Tell fortune by hand**
Dukkering	**Fortune Telling**
Fake	**To Steal**
Fams	**Hands**
Gad	**A Shirt**
Gav	**Place**
Gin/Jin	**Know**
Gorger	**Non Gypsy**
Gravengra	**Doctor**
Gry	**Horse**
Guveni	**Cow**
Habben	**Bread**
Hatch	**Stop**
Hatching Tan	**Stopping Place**
Jukkal	**Dog**
Juvi	**Lousy**
Kair	**To do**
Kaulo	**Black**
Kaulo guery	**Black Man**
Kaulo-Mengro	**Blacksmith**
Kaun	**Ear**
Keir/Kena	**House**
Kek	**No**
Kek Cushty	**No Good**
Kin	**Buy/Take**
Kitchema	**Puplic House**
Kitchema Mengro	**Landlord**
Ladged	**Embarrassed**
Lav	**Name**
Lel/Lelled	**Take/Arrested**
Lende	**You**
Loure	**To Steal**
Luvveny	**Harlot**

Luvver	**Money**
Mai	**Mother**
Mandy	**Me**
Mang	**Talk/Beg**
Manush/Mush	**Man**
Manushi	**Woman**
Mas	**Meat**
Mokkadi	**unclean to eat**
Mort	**Woman**
Motti	**Drunk**
Mui	**Face/Mouth**
Mullered	**Killed/Dead**
Muloh	**Devil**
Muscra	**Police Man**
Muscra's	**Police**
Muter	**Urine**
Mutra Mengri	**Tea**
Narky	**unpleasant**
Nash	**To Run**
Nav/Lav	**Name**
Nok	**Nose**
Odoi	**There**
Olevas	**Legs**
Parno	**White**
Pawni	**Water**
Peave	**Drink**
Peavy	**Drunk**
Peerdie/s	**Foot/Feet**
Poggard	**Broken**
Pogger	**To Break**
Pooker	**To ask/Talk**
Pookering	**Asking/Talking**
Pookering Cosht	**Sign post**
Poove	**Field**
Popin	**Goose**
Potchee/Porashi	**Pocket**
Pramyers	**Trousers**
Putch	**Ask**
Rakli	**Girl**
Rarti	**Night**

Ratt	**Blood**
Rawnie	**Lady**
Rokker	**Speak**
Romanice	**Gypsy Language**
Romany Rye	**Gypsy Gentleman**
Romanychal	**Gypsy Man**
Rommered	**Married**
Rov/	**Cry**
Rovving	**Crying**
Rye	**Gentleman**
Sallakin	**Swearing**
Sastner	**Iron**
Sastner Gry	**Iron Horse/Train**
Scran	**Food**
Shab	**escape**
Shera	**Head**
Shero	**Head**
Shoshoi	**Rabbit**
Staadi	**Hat**
Staripen	**Prison**
Suti	**Sleep**
Tan	**Place**
Tas	**Cup**
Tatti-Pawni	**Hot water**
Ticno	**Child**
Torarti	**tonight**
Traish	**Scare**
Tren	**Three**
Tud	**Milk**
Tugs	**Clothes**
Tuv	**Smoke**
Vardo	**Wagon**
Vast	**Hand**
Vonga	**Money**
Wuddrus	**Bed**
Yari	**Egg**
Yeck	**One**
Yocks/Yacks	**Eyes**
Yog	**Fire**
Yogger	**Gun**